What Lead

MW00990507

"James Goll has done it again. This b
observing at close range the conflict
kingdom of darkness. An essential too~~~~ ~~~ ~~~~~ ~~~~~~~~ ~~ ~~~~~ ~~~~ ~~~~.

—**Mahesh Chavda**, senior pastor, All Nations Church; www.maheshchavda.com

"James Goll is a prophet, teacher, man of integrity, lover of the Bride of
Christ—a man raised in the holiness tradition and a personal friend of mine.
James has the gift of teaching. This is a great addition to the few books that
deal with deliverance. It is thorough in its analysis of demonic activity; biblical
and balanced; practical, positive and powerful. I highly recommend it to anyone
who wants to learn more about the ministry of deliverance."

—**Randy Clark**, founder, Apostolic Network of Global Awakening;
www.globalawakening.com

"James always brings a wealth of wisdom, knowledge and experience to
everything he does. He is both a pragmatist and a practitioner in all he does
in the Holy Spirit."

—**Graham Cooke**, author, *Approaching the Heart of Prophecy* and *Prophecy
and Responsibility*; president, Brilliant Book House; www.grahamcooke.com

"James Goll's *Deliverance from Darkness* is an amazing accomplishment.
It simplifies deliverance concepts for novices and provides seasoned readers
with intriguing insights."

—**Jim Croft**, Jim Croft Ministries; www.thoughtsfromjim.com

"Once again James Goll has made the path clear. He has broken the dynamics
of spiritual warfare and demystified the way to deliverance. He is not giving us
theories. He has survived and risen above personal problems in a most unusual
way. He is a modern-day hero of faith whose example anyone can faithfully
follow. Make this a spiritual guide to transform your life."

—**Bishop Harry R. Jackson Jr.**, senior pastor, Hope Christian Church
(Washington, DC, area); founder and president, High Impact Leadership
Coalition; www.thehopeconnection.org

"James Goll knows how to walk through a firestorm and experience great
freedom and victory. We all need to learn from him."

—**Cindy Jacobs**, co-founder, Generals International; www.generals.org

"The only time I pay attention to the devil is when he gets in my way. There can
be a tendency to give needless attention to the enemy. The call of the Church
is to bring the Kingdom of heaven through the manifested presence of God
to destroy the works of the devil. *Deliverance from Darkness* is an extremely
thorough book needed for this mission. James Goll has skillfully crafted a
book that approaches this subject with authority and delicacy, eliminating
the fear and awe of the enemy, putting the tools of authority into the hands
of believers and fulfilling the mandate of Jesus Christ."

—**Bill Johnson**, senior pastor, Bethel Church (Redding, CA); author, *When
Heaven Invades Earth* and *Face to Face with God*; www.bjm.org

"James Goll is a thorough studier of the Word, an accurate seer prophet, a warrior in the Spirit, a super communicator and full of mercy. *Deliverance from Darkness* is a must-read, a resource you will want to keep in your library. So buy two—one to give away."

—**Patricia King**, president, XPmedia, www.xpmedia.com

"This book is solidly founded in Scripture, which should help even the most profoundly anti-deliverance skeptic reconsider his or her position. We particularly appreciate James' inclusion of steps for deliverance and strong admonishment to extend Kingdom authority over our personal worlds, since our own ministry is directed toward practical how-to's and releasing authority for receiving complete freedom and healing from all of life's wounds."

—**Chester and Betsy Kylstra**, founders,
Restoring the Foundations Ministries; www.rtfi.org

"James Goll's book brings 'biblicity' and balance to a field that can so easily get off track and fall into theological and scriptural error. James writes with simple biblical clarity, lifting the field of deliverance out of the 'weird' practices of a few gifted ones and into the sound province of all in the Church who know Jesus Christ as their personal Lord and Savior."

—**John Loren Sandford**, co-founder, Elijah House; author,
Deliverance and Inner Healing and many others; www.elijahhouse.org

"God is determined to restore Kingdom mentality and, thus, Kingdom life and authority to the Church in the world. He said to Peter, 'I will build My Church and hell cannot stop it.' He also said, 'I give you the keys of the Kingdom.' He also said, 'If I cast out demons by the power of God, the Kingdom has come upon you.' During these days of Kingdom restoration, you will meet the demonic. This book will serve as a valuable resource in setting people free."

—**Jack Taylor**, president, Dimensions Ministries;
www.dimensionsministries.org

"James W. Goll has been recognized as one of the most knowledgeable and experienced spiritual warriors of our generation. His valuable book and study guide will help equip you to confront the enemy on any level, and I hope you will determine to use them to equip others as well. I am so grateful we now have these powerful weapons of spiritual warfare."

—**C. Peter Wagner**, president, Global Harvest Ministries; chancellor,
Wagner Leadership Institute; www.wagnerleadership.org

"James has an amazing grasp of biblical truth, historical knowledge and practical experiential understanding girded with wisdom. He weaves these elements together to help us understand not only the problem but [how to] find the way through to freedom. This book is so helpful, I'm going to keep this book close."

—**Barbara J. Yoder**, senior pastor and lead apostle, Shekinah Christian Church
(Ann Arbor, MI); founder and apostolic leader, Breakthrough Apostolic
Ministries Network; www.shekinahchurch.org

Deliverance *from* Darkness

The Essential Guide to
DEFEATING
Demonic Strongholds
and Oppression

James W. Goll

Chosen

a division of Baker Publishing Group
Grand Rapids, Michigan

© 2010 by James W. Goll

Published by Chosen Books
a division of Baker Publishing Group
P.O. Box 6287, Grand Rapids, MI 49516-6287
www.chosenbooks.com

Printed in the United States of America

All rights reserved. No part of this publication may be reproduced, stored in a retrieval system, or transmitted in any form or by any means—for example, electronic, photocopy, recording—without the prior written permission of the publisher. The only exception is brief quotations in printed reviews.

Library of Congress Cataloging-in-Publication Data
Goll, Jim W.
    Deliverance from darkness : the essential guide to defeating demonic strong-holds and oppression / James W. Goll.
        p.   cm.
    Includes bibliographical references (p.   ) and index.
    ISBN 978-0-8007-9481-1 (pbk.)
    1. Spiritual warfare. I. Title.
BV4509.5.G624 2010
235′.4—dc22   2010015431

Unless otherwise indicated, Scripture is taken from the New King James Version. Copyright © 1982 by Thomas Nelson, Inc. Used by permission. All rights reserved.

Scripture marked NIV is taken from the Holy Bible, New International Version®, NIV®. Copyright © 1973, 1978, 1984 by Biblica, Inc.™ Used by permission of Zondervan. All rights reserved worldwide. www.zondervan.com.

Scriptures marked NASB is taken from the New American Standard Bible®, Copyright © 1960, 1962, 1963, 1968, 1971, 1972, 1973, 1975, 1977, 1995 by The Lockman Foundation. Used by permission.

Scripture marked AMP is taken from the Amplified® Bible, Copyright © 1954, 1958, 1962, 1964, 1965, 1987 by The Lockman Foundation. Used by permission.

Scripture marked KJV is taken from the King James Version of the Bible.

Scripture marked TLB is taken from The Living Bible, copyright © 1971. Used by permission of Tyndale House Publishers, Inc., Wheaton, Illinois 60189. All rights reserved.

10   11   12   13   14   15   16   7   6   5   4   3   2   1

In keeping with biblical principles of creation stewardship, Baker Publishing Group advocates the responsible use of our natural resources. As a member of the Green Press Initiative, our company uses recycled paper when possible. The text paper of this book is comprised of 30% post-consumer waste.

Contents

5

Contents

Foreword

When the charismatic renewal first began in the late 1950s, many of us liberal, old-line, denominational Christians discovered, to our surprise, that demons are real! That was a shock that upset our paradigm of a nice, safe world. For a while, the sector of the Body of Christ of which I was part characteristically ran right off the deep end. Suddenly demons were lurking behind every bush, and we went home looking over our shoulders, just in case. Vomit buckets appeared in many ministry rooms.

A plethora of books came out, many quite good, such as Don Basham's *Deliver Us from Evil*, and some not so good, falling into the Manichaean heresy. More about that in a moment.

Deliverance and inner healing grew up separately, and often antagonistically. Chosen Books asked my son Mark and me to write a book to reconcile the two fields. We planned a seven-chapter book to accomplish that, trying to teach the Church to do both together, neither without the other. In the writing, our editor, Jane Campbell, asked me to include a chapter on delivering places and objects. That grew into another chapter, one about delivering animals as well—which so exploded us out of our original intention that we ending up writing *A Comprehensive Guide to Deliverance and Inner Healing*—emphasis on *comprehensive*.

I say all this to commend James Goll's book as even more comprehensive—and greatly needed by the Body of Christ. It brings biblicity (Mark's note: "Is this a word?") and balance to a field that can so easily get off track and fall into theological and scriptural error. James writes with simple biblical clarity, lifting the field of deliverance out of the "weird" practices of a few gifted ones and into the sound province of all in the Church who know Jesus Christ as their personal Lord and Savior.

Many teachers and some authors who dwell on the subjects of Satan, the kingdom of darkness and the world of the demonic have unwittingly fallen into the heresy of Manichaeism, purporting that life is an eternal battle between good and evil, darkness being God's opposite and almost equal number. The early Church branded that as heresy. The battle is not eternal. Satan is not God's opposite and almost equal number. Life is a good heavenly Father raising sons and daughters for fellowship with Him throughout eternity (see 1 John 1:1–4). There happens to be a war, but it is only one detail in the great tapestry of God's history of redemption through His Son, the Lord Jesus Christ.

In fleshly zeal for the Lord, however, many have tended to get carried away, overemphasizing darkness, and in their writings giving Satan the attention and glory he covets.

James Goll does not fall into that error. Throughout the book he makes clear that God is the Lord and that the earth and all of us belong to Him. Though the book is replete with teaching about how to defeat the devil and cast away his minions, one comes away exalting and exulting in the Lord and His victorious nature, rather than fearing and gearing up in unnecessary tension.

Many teachers and some authors rightly teach how to cast away the demonic—and stop there. James Goll is careful to teach that repentance must follow—as well as precede—deliverance; and that repentance, more than feeling sorry, means so to change one's lifestyle into the way of the Lord Jesus that no demon can return. James Goll carefully teaches righteousness as the guarantee of freedom from the demonic; familiarity with the Word as protection (see Psalm 19, especially verse 11); inner healing as cleansing and transformation so that no demon can find or maintain a lodging place (see, for example, Ephesians 4:26); and the virtue of small groups as the way of victory (see Proverbs 11:14).

Read the book, but do not lay it aside. As a doctor keeps medical manuals handy to refer to while treating patients, keep *Deliverance from Darkness* handy as a resource as you work.

To God be the glory! Remember that as you contest with darkness, and it will flee away.

John Loren Sandford

PART I

The Demonic, Exposed

1

Jesus, Overcoming Demons

Situation: hopeless. The world was like a snake pit. Occupying forces were devouring it piece by piece and soul by soul.

Where was the Messiah? What was taking Him so long?

> Return, we beseech You, O God of hosts;
>   Look down from heaven and see,
>   And visit this vine
> And the vineyard which Your right hand has planted.

Psalm 80:14–15

At last, He came. He came to save—and He came to destroy. Born in Bethlehem and brutally crucified in Jerusalem thirty-odd years later, Jesus Christ came to deliver His beloved world from the destroyer.

To save it, He, too, had to become destructive—Jesus' mission was to obliterate the works of the devil who held His world captive: "For this purpose the Son of God was manifested, that He might destroy the works of the devil" (1 John 3:8).

As He went about preaching and teaching and healing, He turned the enemy's face to the wall. His proclamation, "the Kingdom is here," meant that God had arrived. He had come from heaven to earth to displace the evil forces that had taken over. The Good News became good news only for those who would turn from the darkness of the devil to the Light of Jesus. It became very *bad* news for the prince of darkness, otherwise known as the devil, Satan, the evil one, the prince of demons, the king of the earthly realm.

So with Jesus' birth and later with His baptism in the Jordan River, the Kingdom of God surged into the world, displacing the kingdom of darkness. Too late, the devil discovered that his rulership had come with term limits. Enraged, he renewed his efforts to sack and destroy as much as possible of what God was reclaiming. Meantime, the Son of God calmly and deliberately continued teaching and healing and delivering people from his clutches.

With Jesus' crucifixion, the devil thought he had succeeded in ridding himself of this "usurper" of his long-established reign over the earth. But not for long. After a mere two nights and one full day in the grave, the Son of God rose from the dead, thus annihilating death itself and depriving Satan of what he thought was his ace in the hole.

How Does Jesus Do It?

We need to take a detailed look at the life of Jesus in the New Testament, because He is speaking also to you and me when He tells His disciples, "I say to you, he who believes in Me, the works that I do he will do also; and greater works than these he will do, because I go to My Father" (John 14:12).

You and I have been filled with His Spirit; the Son of God manifests Himself through us today. Therefore, part of our job description is to release His powerful presence into the world where we live, allowing Him to continue to destroy the works of the devil until the job is complete. To do so, we need to examine what it means to overcome the darkness, to take it seriously as a part of our walk of faith, blazing forth His light and vanquishing the darkness, delivering its captives. The question is not only how did Jesus do it when He walked the earth, but also how does He want to continue doing it through people like you and me today?

Jesus in the Wilderness

The Jordan River is the setting for the first New Testament picture of Jesus as an adult. As soon as His cousin John immersed Him in the water of the river, a dove descended upon Him, and the voice of the Father said, "This is My beloved Son, in whom I am well pleased" (Matthew 3:17). In that moment, Jesus became an absolute threat to the powers of darkness.[1]

Straight after being immersed in the water, Jesus was led by the Spirit into the inhospitable desert wilderness of Judea. There, for forty long hungry and thirsty days, the evil one tempted Him with "all that is in the world," as John put it in 1 John 2:16—the lust of the flesh (bread to eat), the lust of the eyes (the miraculous spectacle of defying gravity) and the pride of life (the power and glory of worldly kingdoms). Jesus resisted, successfully, on all three of these "ports of entry." The enemy withdrew from Him for a season to regroup, but the battle was on.

This is always how it works; the devil seeks entry points. He tests and prods, looking for weak places. When he finds one (which he did not, with Jesus), he moves in to see how far he can get.

Sometimes, in the face of an effective rebuke, he will withdraw. What a relief! But it is only one of his schemes to hide for a season, because then people will let their guard down and he can come back when they least expect it. The sounds of battle may fade into the distance from time to time, but the conflict is still on. The Kingdom of light is still being ushered in. The kingdom of darkness is still being vanquished.

Equipped with spiritual weapons and enlisted in the armed forces of God, we need to do our part as fellow soldiers in this ongoing clash. We need to learn all we can from the One who is leading us, the One who holds the keys to victory.

Jesus and the Demons

Soon after coming out of the wilderness, Jesus arrived at the synagogue in Capernaum. As He was teaching—with a level of authority that His listeners recognized as being unusual—a confrontation between kingdoms erupted. Unclean spirits that were present in the person of a demon-possessed man yelled out, "Let us alone! What have we to do with You, Jesus of Nazareth? Did You come to destroy us? I know who You are—the Holy One of God!" (Mark 1:24).

Standing in His unassailable authority, Jesus commanded the demons, "Be quiet! I muzzle and gag you! Come out of this man right now!" (see verse 25). Much to the astonishment of the people in the synagogue, the man was thrown into violent convulsions and then a demon exited with a shriek (see verse 26).

This was no ordinary rabbi! This man simply commanded demons and they left in a hurry. He did not have to resort to magic formulas or conjuring or prolonged coaxing. Completely under the authority of His Father, all He had to do was stand there and raise His voice in a word of command. Apparently the Kingdom of God had just walked into the building, driving out the kingdom of darkness. Later Jesus described it by saying, "If I cast out demons with the finger of God, surely the kingdom of God has come upon you" (Luke 11:20; see also Matthew 12:28).

He had not come with an agenda of His own, but He had been sent to accomplish the will of the Father (see John 7:16–18). He had been sent with an assignment. He had come with a task. And that task was to drive out the kingdom of darkness so that the Kingdom of God could be ushered in.

This was only the first of many such encounters. As Jesus walked from city to city, satanic forces were thrown into an uproar. All He needed to do was to show up for the rule of God to be enforced.

Case Study #1: The Gerasene Demoniac

In college, I was educated as a social worker. That must be why I think the way I do when I read the New Testament; I learned to think in case studies. As a result, when I read an account such as the one in Mark 5 (and the similar one in Matthew 8) about the wild demon-possessed man, I take it apart like a case study.

This is an extreme case if you ever saw one. In every area of this man's life, he was affected by the demons. His social relationships were nonexistent; in fact, people could not even pass near him. Physically, he was always gashing himself on sharp stones and tearing off the shackles and chains that people had tried to subdue him with. Emotionally and mentally, he was out of control. All he could do was shriek out in torment as he crashed around the rough country and in the cemetery where he lived.

Spiritually, however, he was in enough control of himself to want to be set free. "Seeing Jesus from a distance, he ran up and bowed down before Him" (Mark 5:6, NASB). However, immediately upon finding themselves in the actual presence of the Son of God, the demons inside the man made him shout,

"What business do we have with each other, Jesus, Son of the Most High God? I implore you by God, do not torment me!" (Mark 5:7, NASB). They couldn't help it. The manifest presence of God will always cause demons to show themselves, terrified. They shriek loudly. They grovel. They panic. They try evasive tactics.

There were many demons in this man, and one served as the spokesman. Jesus asked, "What is your name?" And he/they said, "My name is Legion; for we are many" (Mark 5:9, NASB).[2] A Roman legion equaled six thousand troops. This legion of demons knew they were about to be evicted. Desperate to dodge the punishment of being cast far away, they begged to be cast into a herd of hogs that was feeding on the hillside. They seemed to be most desperate to stay within the geographical area they knew best, as if being cast out of the region would disorient them and render them ineffective.

Evil spirits need to live in some kind of a body; a body is like a house to them. Preferably, it is a human body so that they can exploit human lusts such as fear, sexual perversion, murder and suicide, but animals will do in a pinch. Notice that when Jesus gave them permission, they swept into the herd of pigs, but they did not enter into any of the human bystanders (see Mark 5:11–13). Upon being commanded to leave, they had to have permission to enter their next hosts. A demon cannot enter anyone without a person's permission and cooperation.

What happened? The utterly destructive nature of the demonic legion caused the entire swine herd, two thousand strong, to rush headlong into the nearby sea, drowning themselves (see verse 13).

And what had happened to the man they used to live in? There he stood, sane and calm, his mental and emotional health completely restored. His sense of dignity had returned. He was so grateful that he wanted to travel with Jesus, but the Lord told him to return to his people instead, and to tell them what had happened to him, which he did, ranging widely among the ten major cities of the region (see Mark 5:18–20). As a result of this one spectacular deliverance, all of the surrounding areas heard about the power of the Kingdom of God, even though Jesus Himself did not stay for very long. In fact, the alarmed swine herdsmen and the people of Gerasa asked Him to leave as soon as possible (see verse 17).

Case Study #2: The Child with an Evil Spirit

This episode is reported in three of the gospels, in Matthew 17:14–21, Mark 9:14–29 and Luke 9:37–42. It happened immediately after the Transfiguration, when Jesus and the three disciples who had been up on the mountain came back down:

> When they came to the other disciples, they saw a large crowd around them and the teachers of the law arguing with them. As soon as all the people saw Jesus, they were overwhelmed with wonder and ran to greet him.
>
> "What are you arguing with them about?" he asked.
>
> A man in the crowd answered, "Teacher, I brought you my son, who is possessed by a spirit that has robbed him of speech. [Other versions say that he was an epileptic.] Whenever it seizes him, it throws him to the ground. He foams at the mouth, gnashes his teeth and becomes rigid. I asked your disciples to drive out the spirit, but they could not."
>
> "O unbelieving generation," Jesus replied, "how long shall I stay with you? How long shall I put up with you? Bring the boy to me."
>
> So they brought him. When the spirit saw Jesus, it immediately threw the boy into a convulsion. He fell to the ground and rolled around, foaming at the mouth.
>
> Jesus asked the boy's father, "How long has he been like this?"

"From childhood," he answered. "It has often thrown him into fire or water to kill him. But if you can do anything, take pity on us and help us."

"'If you can'?" said Jesus. "Everything is possible for him who believes."

Immediately the boy's father exclaimed, "I do believe; help me overcome my unbelief!"

When Jesus saw that a crowd was running to the scene, he rebuked the evil spirit. "You deaf and mute spirit," he said, "I command you, come out of him and never enter him again."

The spirit shrieked, convulsed him violently and came out. The boy looked so much like a corpse that many said, "He's dead." But Jesus took him by the hand and lifted him to his feet, and he stood up.

After Jesus had gone indoors, his disciples asked him privately, "Why couldn't we drive it out?"

He replied, "This kind can come out only by prayer."

Mark 9:14–29, NIV

Notice several things about this story. One, as in the case of the Gerasene demoniac, when Jesus approached, the demons reacted. In this case, the deaf and mute spirit (as he later calls it) threw the boy into a convulsion on the spot. If nothing else, this is a diversionary tactic designed to instill fear and dissipate faith.

Two, note that this evil spirit affected the boy in every way: physically, socially, mentally, emotionally and spiritually. He could not live a normal life. Neither could his family. They had run out of options, and if Jesus' own disciples could not cast out what was obviously an evil spirit, what more could they do?

Three, the boy's father had enough faith to bring his son to the disciples and then, of course, to Jesus. He was honest about his level of faith. Naturally, it had been shaken with repeated failures. But he had enough faith to ask the Lord to remedy his lack of faith, and that was enough.

Four, when Jesus questioned the father about how long he had been afflicted in this way, we can see that even Jesus did not always operate on a gift of knowledge about past and future circumstances. Sometimes, as we certainly need to do, He needed to get background information by asking questions. It was like a short interview. His questions also demonstrated to the father of the boy that He was interested in both of them and that He was not too self-important to get involved in their problems.

Five, from talking with the father of the boy, Jesus knew that this spirit was trying to destroy him, and how it was operating. However, nobody seems to have told Him that the boy was deaf and mute. And yet when He named the spirit to cast it out, He said, "You deaf and mute spirit, I command you, come out of him and never enter him again." This additional dimension of the demon's activity was revealed to Jesus directly by the Spirit.

A sixth observation is an interesting one: When Jesus saw a crowd coming to see what was happening, He quickly cast the spirit out of the boy. Why didn't He wait until the crowd got there? You would think He would have wanted more people to witness the deliverance.

We can only surmise that the presence of the "gawkers" would have inhibited the process. Perhaps that would have given unnecessary extra attention to the evil spirit. Perhaps Jesus wanted to avoid the heightened emotion of a crowd mentality, which could cause faith to disappear in the face of conflicting human emotions. Perhaps He simply wanted to protect the boy from feeling like a freak in a sideshow. In any case, it was a good thing to do.

This account from Mark lays good emphasis on the father's faithful response to Jesus. This, too, is informative for us. Not only can we see the importance of a faith-filled response to God's power in this one situation, but we see how Jesus broadens it to apply to every other situation when He says, "Everything is possible for him who believes." Like the father of the boy, most of us want to reach out our hands saying, "I do believe, but please help my faltering faith."

Last, note that, although the demon did not leave without a struggle and loud objections, it did leave quite promptly when Jesus commanded it to go and never return. Jesus' authority is absolute. Even rebellious evil spirits must obey His word of command.

Jesus modeled for us His heart of compassion when He helped the traumatized boy up to his feet and restored him to his father, who was probably weeping by then. Jesus always strengthens us. His love is expressed in the most practical terms: healing, deliverance and restoration. He also modeled for us a profound respect for parental authority. All the way through this event, He deferred to the boy's father, and He returned the boy to his dad at the end. We should be the same way, respecting the parental authority over any children we may minister to.

Case Study #3: The Man with the Unclean Spirit

Of the four gospels, the book of Mark is the one that has the fullest accounts of demonic confrontations and what John Wimber called "power encounters." Early in this chapter, I mentioned Jesus' visit to the synagogue in Capernaum. Mark and Luke both included the same details of this story (see Mark 1:21–28 and Luke 4:31–37).

Apparently it was Jesus' *authority* that stood out. Whatever He was teaching about must have been much like what the scribes always taught, but His presence was arrestingly different. In this case, the demonized man seems to have been behaving normally—until Jesus displayed His authority in His teaching. Then the unclean spirit made the man shout aloud (see Mark 1:24; Luke 4:34), questioning Jesus' authority. The demon seemed to recognize that Jesus had come to deprive him of his host, even to destroy him. Jesus silenced the unclean spirit and commanded it to leave. Defying the command to be quiet, the demon caused convulsions and ear-splitting shrieks as he left, but he did not harm the man: "All the people were amazed and said to each other, 'What is this teaching? With authority and power he gives orders to evil spirits and they come out!' And the news about him spread throughout the surrounding area" (Luke 4:36–37, NIV; see also Mark 1:27–28). The salient features of this episode are: (1) the compelling authority of Jesus, and (2) the resulting widespread news about Him.

Case Study #4: The Syrophoenician Woman's Daughter

When Jesus came into the coastal region in northern Israel, His reputation must have preceded Him. One of the native Canaanites from that Gentile region of the ancient Phoenician capital cities of Tyre and Sidon, a woman, was bold enough (and desperate enough) to come to Him on behalf of her demon-possessed daughter (see Matthew 15:22–28 and Mark 7:24–30).

The account does not tell the nature of the girl's demonization, but it does indicate that the daughter was many miles away, at home, while her mother sought Jesus out. Amazingly persistent, even in the face of Jesus' repudiation, this mother was shameless, branding herself as a "dog" if only Jesus would fulfill her request. She knew He could do it; the question was whether or not He *would* do it.

Jesus was impressed. This woman's faith was remarkable. He declared (no loud commands needed here) the girl's deliverance: "For such a reply, you may go; the demon has left your daughter" (Mark 7:29, NIV). Hurrying back to her home, the woman found her daughter lying in bed, healed and restored.

This account shows us that Jesus' authority is boundless. Not only did He pronounce immediate deliverance on a child from another culture that was not part of the children of Israel, but the deliverance was effective over a long distance. He never saw the girl, and she never saw Him. At the same time, Jesus respected the natural parental authority of the woman. He certainly would not have performed a long-distance deliverance on this little girl without her mother's earnest invitation.

More Case Studies

Wherever Jesus went, crowds gathered. Demoniacs were often healed in those crowds. In some cases, the demons became disruptive (see Mark 3:10–11 and Luke 4:41; see also Acts 8:7, where demons shrieked in Philip's large meetings as they were driven out of people).

Most of the time, Jesus commanded the unclean spirits not to reveal His identity:

> When evening came, after the sun had set, they began bringing to Him all who were ill and those who were demon-possessed. And the whole city had gathered at the door. And He healed many who were ill with various diseases, and cast out many demons; and He was not permitting the demons to speak, because they knew who He was.
>
> Mark 1:32–34, NASB

Regardless of the behavior of the demons, Jesus drove them out with as little as a single word (see Matthew 8:16). He also healed people who were "troubled by evil spirits" (Luke 6:18, NIV). This seems to imply a lesser degree of demonic influence—"affliction" or "oppression" as opposed to "control" or "possession."

Looking at all of the case studies, including those that involve Jesus' disciples, we can observe at least six different ways that evil spirits can be compelled to leave people alone:

1. By the command of faith (see Mark 1:25; 9:25)
2. Through the laying on of hands (see Luke 4:40–41)
3. Through anointing with oil (see Mark 6:12–13)
4. By exposure to Jesus' authority (see Mark 5:6–7; 9:20)
5. Through a verbal expression of faith[3] (see Matthew 15:28 and Mark 7:29)
6. By means of prayer and fasting (see Matthew 17:21)

As Jesus' modern-day disciples, whenever we encounter demons or unclean spirits we can use any of these means of deliverance, as His Spirit leads. Jesus has demonstrated for us what to do. We must take what we know and use it to further the spread of His Kingdom and the ongoing destruction of the works of the devil.

Characteristics of Demons in the New Testament

These case studies, or snapshots, of Jesus' ministry reveal the modus operandi of demons, as well as the basic components of their personalities.

Three elements of personality characterize demons: (1) They have a degree of knowledge (see Mark 1:24: "I know who You are"); (2) they have a will (see Matthew 12:44 and Isaiah 14:13–14[4]); and (3) they have emotions—all negative ones (see Mark 1:26; 5:7; 9:26). After all, they do believe in the surpassing power of the Lord Jesus (see James 2:19[5]). They take their knowledge of the truth and they twist it. Demons share the characteristics of the father of lies, Beelzebub. They are stubborn at times and must be overcome with proper preparation and persistent effort (see Mark 5:8; 9:26–29).

As we saw in the story of the Gerasene demoniac, they prefer to inhabit and torment human beings, but rather than wandering around without a body, they will settle for occupying the body of an animal. Besides calling the bodies they inhabit "my house" (see Matthew 12:44; Luke 11:24), demons also seem to have assigned territories. They prefer to stay in the country or region they currently reside in than to be banished (see Mark 5:10). In Daniel 10:13, we can clearly see a territorial assignment. Whenever they lack a lodging place, they are restless (see Matthew 12:43).

Demonic beings are ranked according to levels of wickedness: "Then he goes and takes with him seven other spirits more wicked than himself" (Matthew 12:45). Commonly they are named by the way they defile, afflict, tempt or torment. Jesus used the common designation of "foul" or "unclean" spirits, and this term covered everything from the legion of demons in Mark 5 to spirits causing sickness (see Luke 9:42) and spirits of war (see Revelation 16:13–14).

Other New Testament names for evil spirits include "dumb spirit" or "mute spirit" (Mark 9:17), "deaf and dumb spirit" or "deaf and mute spirit" (Mark 9:25), "spirit of infirmity" (Luke 13:11), a "spirit of divination" (Acts 16:16), a "spirit of bondage" or "spirit of slavery" (Romans 8:15), the "spirit of the world" (1 Corinthians 2:12), "seducing" or "deceiving spirits" (1 Timothy 4:1), a "spirit of disobedience" (see Ephesians 2:2), and "the spirit of the Antichrist" (1 John 4:3).

Jesus dominates all demonic powers from His position at the right hand of the Father, where He waits until all the remaining rebels are brought into subjection under His feet (see 1 Corinthians 15:20–25). When He appeared to His disciples after His resurrection, He said, "All authority has been given to Me in heaven and on earth. Go therefore . . ." (Matthew 28:18–19, NASB). No longer does the earth belong to Satan, because Jesus has regained control of the earth from the prince of the world system. Now He has sent His disciples into the world as ambassadors of heaven to proclaim and reveal His Lordship (see Mark 16:15 and 2 Corinthians 5:20).

He said that the first sign of authenticity of those who go forth proclaiming would be that they would cast out demons in His name (see Mark 16:15–17). Casting out demons thus becomes an important component of our marching orders, and that is why a book such as this one is a valuable tool for our arsenal.

2

Overcoming Demons in the Early Church

When Jesus uttered, "It is finished!" He overturned the very foundation of satanic rule on earth. That foundation, established before human memory through pride, rebellion, disobedience, deceit, darkness and destruction, could no longer resist when the Son of God humbled Himself to death.

It was more than the completion of Jesus' life on earth; it was the culmination of an old regime. Darkness had lost. Light had prevailed. The veil between heaven and earth had been torn in two along with the Temple veil (see Matthew 27:51; Mark 15:38; Luke 23:45). Nothing would ever be the same again.

From that point on, God could usher people into Paradise, starting with the repentant thief (see Luke 23:43). The angelic guard at the Tree of Life could now admit all who repented and believed in the Son (see Genesis 3:24; Revelation 22:14).

On the third day, when Jesus reclaimed His Spirit and stood up in His grave, He initiated a new phase of the campaign to regain the fallen world. Appearing to His disciples after His resurrection, He said, "All authority has been given to Me in heaven and on earth. Go therefore and make disciples of all the nations . . . and lo, I am with you always, even to the end of the age" (Matthew 28:18–20). No longer did the nations belong to Satan. Jesus had regained the entire earth from the prince of the world system. As He sat down at the right hand of His Father, His disciples remained on the earth as His ambassadors, proclaiming and revealing His Lordship. Fifty days later, He bestowed His Spirit upon them on Pentecost, and the Church was born (see Acts 2).

The Demon-Defying Acts of the Apostles

The new Church had a lot of overcoming to do. At first, along with thousands of converts, such a tidal wave of grace and power seemed to flow out from Jerusalem that the first four chapters of the book of Acts seem to portray a taste of millennial life. Harmony and healings, charisma and community enabled the multitude to take root and bear fruit quickly.

Then came the shocking first mention of satanic backlash, the account of the married couple who agreed to lie to the Holy Spirit about how much money they were donating to the community of faith (see Acts 5:1–10).

Ananias and Sapphira

Ananias and Sapphira appeared to be members of the apostolic community in good standing. To keep for themselves some of the proceeds from selling their land would have been all right. But instead of being honest about it, they decided to lie to the apostles. Oh, it was just a white lie, right? They merely exaggerated the amount a bit when they said, "We are giving everything."

Why did they do that? Were they feeling insecure about their status? Trying to earn favor? Vying for a position of authority?

We do not know. Their deception, the apostle Peter told them, was due to Satan filling their hearts (see Acts 5:3). This is a telling statement. They had experienced grace, and yet they had not guarded their hearts with vigilance against a new incursion of the enemy. Satan had prowled around like a roaring lion, seeking a new stronghold, and he had discovered an entry point. He had not merely planted thoughts into their minds, he had filled their hearts, deadened their consciences and warped their wills.

To avoid setting a dangerous precedent in the Church, the Lord judged these two with severity—he struck them dead (see Acts 5:5, 10). Terrifying! The message could not be clearer. Luke ended that story with the statement: "Great fear came upon all the church and upon all who heard these things" (Acts 5:11).

The resulting fear of the Lord produced new purity and greater intensity in the evangelistic outreach of the Church. Now Jesus' prediction was starting to come true; "greater works" than those of Jesus began to occur. Even Peter's passing shadow brought healing and deliverance to the people it fell upon (see Acts 5:15).

But now that they were being dealt with directly—Satan and his demons struck back, stirring up severe persecution. For example, whereas before they had been given a verbal reprimand, now the apostles were imprisoned and then beaten and flogged for preaching the Good News (see the rest of Acts 5).

Stephen and Philip

Even greater persecution arose after the gifted deacon Stephen exposed the hypocrisy of the religious system and was martyred for it (see Acts 7). The Church was hounded out of town, leaving behind only a remnant of its members. But as the believers scattered abroad, the burning proclamation of Jesus scattered like embers on dry grass. The fire of the Kingdom was spreading.

In Samaria all Philip had to do was to proclaim Christ crucified and unclean spirits came out of people:

31

Therefore those who were scattered went everywhere preaching the word. Then Philip went down to the city of Samaria and preached Christ to them. And the multitudes with one accord heeded the things spoken by Philip, hearing and seeing the miracles which he did. For unclean spirits, crying with a loud voice, came out of many who were possessed; and many who were paralyzed and lame were healed. And there was great joy in that city.

Acts 8:4–8

The simple proclamation of Jesus Christ—that was all it took to drive the demons out of their hiding places in the citizens, with restoration and healing following.

The Slave Girl

A woman named Lydia was the apostolic doorkeeper for a whole continent. In response to his "Macedonian call," Paul traveled to Philippi (see Acts 16:9–12). There he and his companions met Lydia, who was a prominent woman and a merchant. She listened to Paul and she believed the Gospel. After she and her household had been baptized, she invited Paul and the other missionaries to stay at her house. This gave them a base of operations in Philippi. That is how they encountered the slave girl who was a fortune-teller (see Acts 16:16–19).

It was just a chance encounter—or was it? The girl could predict the future because she had an evil spirit of divination, and her owners were exploiting her for financial gain. This evil spirit knew that these men belonged to Jesus and were filled with His Holy Spirit. In other words, Paul and Silas and the others were known in the demonic world.[1]

The spirit caused the girl to trail along with Paul's party for days on end, announcing loudly and often: "These men are the servants of the Most High God, who proclaim to us the way of salvation" (Acts 16:17). This was like a demonic word of knowledge. It was also false flattery, unhelpful advertising for the missionary team and a continual distraction for the men. Like a horsefly, the spirit pestered and harassed them whenever they stepped into the street. The words sounded right. These men *were* servants of the Most High God, proclaiming the way of salvation. But the Greek word that is used here for "divination" is the word *puthon* (like "python"). Like a pagan oracle or a snake, the evil one was squeezing the life out of the truth. So much religious verbiage was making it hard for the team to hear the Spirit and for the people to hear the message that they were proclaiming. Paul became greatly annoyed.

Notice that Paul showed patience—for days on end—before he acted. Most likely, he was discerning and waiting for the appropriate moment. He did not want to act out of his natural impetuousness or irritation. Suddenly, he reached a tipping point: "Paul, greatly annoyed, turned and said to the spirit, 'I command you in the name of Jesus Christ to come out of her.' And he came out that very hour" (Acts 16:18). Paul did not address the girl, who was being victimized; he addressed the spirit of divination. The slave girl was free at last.

The rest of the city was not free, however. In fact, dark spiritual powers seemed to hold much power over the culture and commerce of the region. The deliverance of one little girl was disruptive to the system. An unexpectedly violent reaction followed. The slave owners seized Paul and Silas and dragged them to the marketplace to confront the magistrates. A large mob gathered against them. The magistrates tore off Paul and Silas's clothes and commanded them to be beaten with rods, after which they threw them into prison and put them in stocks (see Acts 16:19–24).

Paul and Silas were imprisoned—temporarily, as it turned out—but their message was unshackled. Instead of sinking into a religious stupor, the region of Philippi heard the Good News and responded. The darkness retreated. The Church spread.

The Ephesian Revival

Paul and the disciples traveled to Ephesus, where they stayed for more than two years, preaching and establishing the local church (see Acts 19:1–10). After the initial growth of the church, an additional level of grace was released through Paul (see Acts 19:11–20). The anointing of the Holy Spirit was manifested in new ways—through cloths that had touched Paul's body. When the cloths touched people, sicknesses and demons departed as if Paul had touched them personally.

This demonstrates how demons can be forced out through a point of contact, which in this case was an anointed piece of cloth. More commonly the point of contact happens through the laying on of hands (see Luke 4:40–41 for the first example in Scripture) or through anointing the sick with oil (see Mark 6:13).

Some Jewish exorcists tried to get in on the act, invoking "the name of Jesus whom Paul preaches." They suffered a humiliating public failure (see Acts 19:13–16), after which the Church grew even more. Persecution reached new heights as well, with the riot and near-lynching over the goddess Artemis (see Acts 19:23–41). The disciples knew that as they pressed forward, preaching the Gospel and destroying the works of the enemy, persecution would continue to come along with success.

Acts of Power

Throughout the book of Acts, whenever the Lordship of Jesus Christ was proclaimed, demons were vanquished. Peter, Philip, Paul and unnamed others clearly demonstrated that because of Jesus' ascension and His bestowal of the Holy Spirit on the Church, demons must yield. Whenever and wherever they encountered the disciples, demons fled. The same dynamic is true today. Whenever demons encounter disciples who have submitted to the rulership of Jesus Christ, they must flee in the face of commands, proclamations, prayers and human lives submitted to the Spirit.

The Name is what does it. Just as the Roman magistrates' authority was backed by the name of Caesar and all his imperial armies (see Acts 16:38), so one individual disciple of Jesus Christ is backed by legions of angels, not to mention the Father, Son and Holy Spirit.

This represents a whole new power equation, one in which you and I participate to this day.

Spiritual Warfare in the Epistles

The epistles (the book of Romans through the short book of Jude) were letters written to various individuals and local churches. That explains why they do not contain extensive portrayals of deliverance.

After all, in the early Church, the norm was to get rid of demons between the time of conversion and baptism. The best defense being a good offense, the question after baptism was no longer how to get them out but how to *keep* them out through holy living—prayer, obedience to God and good deeds. Thus, holy living is the primary topic of the epistles.

Throughout the epistles, any discussion of spiritual warfare occurs in the larger context of practical exhortations and instructions about how to live a holy life in the power of the Holy Spirit. Warnings about the evil one fit into this context.

The Wrestling Match

One of the longest discussions about spiritual warfare in the epistles is in the sixth chapter of the book of Ephesians. Paul pictures a wrestling match with "persons without bodies" (Ephesians 6:12, TLB).

> Finally, my brethren, be strong in the Lord and in the power of His might. Put on the whole armor of God, that you may be able to stand against the wiles of the devil. For we do not wrestle against flesh and blood, but against principalities, against powers, against the rulers of the darkness of this age, against spiritual hosts of wickedness in the heavenly places.
>
> Ephesians 6:10–12

These persons without bodies are evil spirits of varying descriptions.

Principalities are ruling spirits who have been assigned to particular spheres of influence. In geopolitical terms, we use the word *principality* to describe a place such as Monaco that is ruled by a prince. In spiritual terms, a principality rules over a jurisdiction as small as one human body or as large as a nation or region. Evil principalities are princes, with many subordinate spirits under them.

Powers (literally, "authorities") are the realms of authority in which the ruling princes operate. For example the realm of authority of the spiritual "prince of Persia" (see Daniel 10:13) was the kingdom of Persia. (The angel Michael, mentioned in that same passage, is also a prince, one of the chief princes of God's angelic army. He came in response to Daniel's prayers to fight against the evil prince of Persia.)

The *rulers of darkness of this world* indicate the heinous henchmen of our adversary, the devil. These spirits dominate the world system by force and they operate behind the scenes in every era. Picture a dark "SS," or spiritual "Gestapo," controlling other demons and angels with fear, torture and brute force.

The phrase *spiritual wickedness in high places* paints a picture of hosts of evil in the unseen realm—countless foot soldiers that are under the control of Satan, his fallen angelic princes and his world dominators. These foot-soldier demons are lower spirits that have established strongholds in individuals, families, neighborhoods and cities (see 2 Corinthians 10:3–6). All evil powers have a legal right to exercise their authority in their realm. This is why it is so important to keep yourself wholly submitted to God and His earthly representatives (see Ephesians 5–6; 1 Peter 2, 4, 5:9).[2] In guarding and warring against evil powers, our best defense is holy living, which keeps us from having "chinks in our armor" that the enemy can exploit.

Why should the rebel Satan submit to me if I am in rebellion myself? Even in speaking about higher spiritual powers, Christians were warned not to slander or revile but rather to be respectful (see 2 Peter 2:10–11; Jude 9–10). Peter gave insights about submission in his first epistle, urging submission to governmental authorities (see 1 Peter 2:14–18), family authorities (see 1 Peter 3:1–7) and Church authorities (see 1 Peter 5:1–6), because of what is happening spiritually, behind the scenes. Peter learned about submission from firsthand experience.

Peter contrasts suffering for disobedience with suffering for obedience (see 1 Peter 2:19–20). Even when we are obeying and submitting to earthly authorities, evil spirits will stir them up to oppose us, causing us to suffer. When that happens, we are following in Jesus' steps (see 1 Peter 2:21–23). For every blow or mistreatment they cause, the evil ones are destroying their own kingdom. In such times of suffering, the spirit of glory and of God rests on us (see 1 Peter 4:14). God releases new angels to come and assist us in the battle, and the powers of darkness lose again (see Matthew 4:11; Luke 22:43–44). Suffering submissively is a powerful weapon in taking ground from the enemy's camp.

On the other hand, if we walk in rebellion and disobedience to earthly authority, we open the door to the kingdom of darkness, bringing suffering and judgment against ourselves (see Romans 13:2). Thus Peter's admonition, "It is better, if it is God's will, to suffer for doing good than for doing evil" (1 Peter 3:17, NIV).[3]

As it is, if we submit to God, then we can resist the devil effectively and he will flee from us. You might think that you are getting somewhere by casting out a few minor demons in Jesus' name while living a life of lying, lawlessness and rebellion, but remember Jesus' sober warning:

> Not everyone who says to Me, "Lord, Lord," shall enter the kingdom of heaven, but he who does the will of My Father in heaven. Many will say to Me in that day, "Lord, Lord, have we not prophesied in Your name, cast out demons in Your name, and done many wonders in Your name?" And then I will declare to them, "I never knew you; depart from Me, you who practice lawlessness!"
>
> Matthew 7:21–23

As we submit to Jesus in the intimate love of the Bride of Christ, He causes us to rise up as part of a victorious army. Paul first depicted the Bride of Christ (see Ephesians 5:22–33), followed by army warfare (see Ephesians 6:10–18).

When you were born again into the Kingdom of God, you were born in a war zone. Therefore, you were born *to* war. You cannot escape it. For your own protection and for the sake of the Gospel, you need to learn all you can about how to war and wrestle with evil forces.

Always Watchful

After talking about our spiritual wrestling match in Ephesians 6:10–12, Paul goes on to describe the spiritual armor that every believer should be wearing at all times, each piece of armor corresponding to an offensive or defensive weapon (see Ephesians 6:13–18).

In his second epistle to the church at Corinth, Paul explained more about how we do not fight with fists and guns, but rather with spiritual weapons. Once demons no longer have their residence inside a person, the primary arena of warfare will be in the person's mind, which is where old ways of thinking may have become strongholds. Lines of reasoning may have become habitual that seem logical but are rooted in human pride and strength. Thus Paul writes:

> The weapons we fight with are not the weapons of the world. On the contrary, they have divine power to demolish strongholds. We demolish arguments and every pretension that sets itself up against the knowledge of God, and we take captive every thought to make it obedient to Christ.
>
> 2 Corinthians 10:4–5, NIV

How do you "take captive every thought"? You can capture your thoughts much as a watchful guard would say, "Halt! Who goes there?" and then examine the interloper. You lay hold of your thought and you find out its place of origin. Does it acknowledge Jesus' Lordship and further His Kingdom? Or does it hinder? When you discover a thought that has been sent by the enemy, turn it over to Jesus in prayer.

Many of us live compromised lives. We keep one foot in each kingdom. If this were Judgment Day, we would be in serious trouble. Paul wanted to make sure that everyone who names the name of Jesus lives an uncompromised life:

The hour has come for you to wake up from your slumber, because our salvation is nearer now than when we first believed. The night is nearly over; the day is almost here. So let us put aside the deeds of darkness and put on the armor of light. Let us behave decently, as in the daytime, not in orgies and drunkenness, not in sexual immorality and debauchery, not in dissension and jealousy. Rather, clothe yourselves with the Lord Jesus Christ, and do not think about how to gratify the desires of the sinful nature.

Romans 13:11–14, NIV

Stay watchful to stay free. The enemy will continue to prowl around "like a roaring lion, seeking someone to devour" (1 Peter 5:8, NASB)—but he doesn't have to devour you!

How to Stay Free

Godly character is one of the highest weapons of spiritual warfare. God wants us to have not only supernatural power but also supernatural character. Allowing the Holy Spirit to shape our character traits and habits brings us into alignment with the Kingdom so that our spiritual victory is assured.

Righteousness is both an offensive and a defensive weapon. At the end of his letter to the Romans, Paul wrote, "I want you to be wise in what is good and innocent in what is evil. The God of peace will soon crush Satan under your feet" (Romans 16:19–20, NASB). When he encounters righteousness, Satan's face gets smashed into the dirt.

To stay free of Satan's snares, we must: (1) Practice forgiveness regularly (see 2 Corinthians 2:6–11; Colossians 3:13); (2) behave as humble servants of others and of God (see 1 Peter 5:5–7); (3) overcome evil by doing good (see Romans 12:21); (4) focus our thoughts on things that are godly and uplifting (see Colossians 3:1–2; Philippians 4:8–9) and (5) live obedient lives (see Titus 3:1–3; Romans 13:1–2). Nobody can live a righteous life without supernatural help. With the day and night help of the Holy Spirit, we can only pull it off.

Consistent praise, prayer, rejoicing and thankfulness enable us to hold our faith shields steady (see Ephesians 6:16; Philippians 4:4–7; 1 Thessalonians 5:16–18; Hebrews 13:15). In addition to the shield of faith, the rest of the armor of God—the belt of truth, the breastplate of righteousness, the helmet of salvation and the shoes of the gospel of peace (see Ephesians 6:13–18)—protects your front side, but not your back. That is because we are always on the offense. We are never to run from the enemy.

The Word of God and prayer are two weapons that can serve in hand-to-hand combat as well as global offensive strategies. John Wesley referred to the "weapon of all-prayer," which enables us to go on the offensive all over the world, led by our guide, the Holy Spirit. Paul also spoke of the armor of light (see Romans 13:12). Simply walking in the open light with Christ and the Body of Christ can be one of the greatest defenses against demon activity (see 1 John 1:7).

Warnings on Continued Watchfulness

Jesus warned that an unclean spirit, upon returning to his former house and finding it neat and empty, would reenter it with seven other spirits more wicked than himself (see Matthew 12:43–45). He was sounding a warning: When demons have been evicted, replace them with the Holy Spirit, the Word of God and righteous virtues. Fill the place with light. Saturate it and permeate it with worship and faith.

Paul warned against opening the door of your house to religious spirits, who will not be afraid to come knocking. Religious, legalistic spirits may seem friendly, but allowing them to come in may result in a revival of old bondages, fears and deceits. Paul spoke of such things in many of his letters (see Romans 8:15; Galatians 3:1, 4:3, 5:19–21; Colossians 2:20, 3:5–9).

Paul also warned of deceitful, seducing spirits carrying "doctrines of demons," coming to summon and accuse believers, luring them to depart from the faith (see 1 Timothy 4:1–3). James spoke of believers harboring bitter envy and self-seeking in their hearts. He identified this "wisdom" as demonic in its source (see James 3:14–15). John spoke of the spirit of antichrist that would try to lead people away from Christ (see 1 John 2:18–24; 4:1–3).

All of these things were spoken and written to born-again, Spirit-filled believers like you and me. Simply stepping into the Light does not keep you there. Anytime you allow yourself to edge into the darkness, the enemy is right there, looking for his opportunity. Demons have the legal right to operate in the realm of darkness. If Christians, even after having been delivered of demonic influences, go back to walking in the darkness of sinful patterns, they open themselves again to demonic access.

The call of the apostles was to "stand fast therefore in the liberty by which Christ has made us free, and do not be entangled again with a yoke of bondage" (Galatians 5:1). Once a person has been set free, he or she must stay free by putting into practice the life of the Son of God.

The letters that we can read in the New Testament teach us in very practical ways how to occupy the land we have taken from Satan through our Lord Jesus Christ, and how to make it bear fruit for God. Each of us has become a soldier in God's army, waging a love war and bringing many others from the authority of darkness into the Kingdom of God's beloved Son (see Colossians 1:13).

Overcoming in the Book of Revelation

The last book of the Bible paints one of the most encouraging pictures of victory in the entire Bible: the Lamb's final victory over Satan. The entire book reflects the understanding of the early Church regarding overcoming demonic forces in all of their guises:

1. Demons are being worshiped when idols are worshiped (see Revelation 9:20).
2. Pagan religions are manifestations of Satan (see Revelation 2:13).
3. False teachings are inspired by Satan (see Revelation 2:24).
4. The devil motivates the persecution and martyrdom of Christians (see Revelation 2:10).
5. Satan is the ruler behind the scenes for the Antichrist (see Revelation 13:1–14; 19:19).
6. Demons are released to torment men (see Revelation 9:2–11).
7. Demons motivate and encourage war (see Revelation 16:13–14).

Demons had filled the religious and political system called Babylon (see Revelation 18:2). Babylon is a "type" (a foreshadowing) of the world system, organized independent of God with Satan at its head.

The Blood

What makes it possible for the saints of God to overcome Satan and his fallen angels? First of all, it is the blood of the Lamb of God, Jesus, followed by "the word of their testimony" and not loving their lives unto death (see Revelation 12:11).

The blood of Jesus, shed for our sins on the cross, "speaks better things than that of Abel" (see Hebrews 12:24). It cries for mercy on our behalf, not judgment. By the blood of Jesus, we have been redeemed from Satan (see Ephesians 1:7; Psalm 106:10). We have been forgiven because of the shed blood of Jesus, and our forgiveness removes Satan's basis for accusation (see Ephesians 1:7; Colossians 2:13).

By the blood of Jesus, we have been justified (see Romans 5:9, 14). As Derek Prince used to say, being justified means it is "just-as-if-I'd never sinned." By His blood, we have been sanctified, made holy, set apart to God (see Hebrews 13:12). By His blood, heaven has been opened, all the way to the very throne of the Father, so that we can come and have intimate fellowship with Him (see Hebrews 9:22–24; 10:19–22).

Surely the blood of Jesus prevails in every way over the works of darkness.

The Word of Testimony

What else prevails over the works of the devil? The word of our testimony. This one requires a little explanation.

A testimony is given by a witness. The word for "witness" in Greek is *martus*, from which we get our English word "martyr." The word implies that one who will testify to Jesus' sacrifice on the cross would be willing to speak about it even if that costs him his life.

The example given in the book of Revelation is Antipas, known as "my faithful martyr" (Revelation 2:13) or "my faithful witness" (NIV). Other witness-martyrs include John the Baptist, Stephen, and all of the apostles.[4]

When a believer courageously speaks out about his faith, the powers of darkness are pushed back as with a sword of the Spirit (see Ephesians 6:17). Sometimes blood will be shed.

Not Loving Our Lives unto Death

Closely linked with the blood of Jesus and the word of our testimony is the idea of not loving our lives too much, even if it means death. For spiritual soldiers, the willingness to die is a prerequisite. For believers, this begins with the willingness to take up his cross and to die daily (see 1 Corinthians 15:31). Paul said that he did not count his life as dear to himself (see Acts 20:24). This is the way of the Lamb, lived out in His Church. The apostolic Gospel of the Kingdom involves an empowering baptism in the Holy Spirit. When Jesus told the disciples, "You will receive power when the Holy Spirit has come upon you; and you shall be My witnesses" (Acts 1:8, NASB), He meant that they would have power not only to dethrone evil forces, but also to enforce their dethronement and to maintain their own liberty, even if it required their own physical death. Once someone considers him- or herself dead with Christ, that person is truly free.

In the seventeenth chapter of the book of Revelation, the destruction of Babylon proceeds from the blood of the saints and martyrs of Jesus. From this we see that the blood of the Lamb, which speaks in heaven, also flows through His Body (the Church) on earth. When a martyr is slain, it is Jesus' blood that is flowing afresh. One more time, the judgments of God are being loosed against the demons who caused a saint to die.

We do not like to hear this message. We would prefer to think that Jesus' name is like a rabbit foot or a lucky charm. Instead, the apostolic Gospel of the Kingdom involves blood and the willingness to shed blood. God's greatest weapons against demonic powers include disciples who are fully yielded to the Spirit and who have no other agenda besides doing the will of the Father.

The Prayer of the Lord

From beginning to end, the New Testament covers the subject of overcoming demonic powers. By the time we get to the book of Revelation, we find out how it will all end, with Satan being judged (see John 16:11) and cast into the lake of fire along with his legions (see Revelation 20:10, 14–15; Matthew 25:40–41).

The beautiful, submissive Bride will become part of the victorious army that will return with the Lamb, who is also the Lion of God, when He comes to set up His never-ending Kingdom. With Him, we can pray with new vigor:

> Thy kingdom come, Thy will be done in earth, as it is in heaven.
> Give us this day our daily bread.
> And forgive us our debts, as we forgive our debtors.
> And lead us not into temptation, but deliver us from evil: For thine is the kingdom, and the power, and the glory, for ever. Amen.
>
> Matthew 6:10–13, KJV

3

Scriptural Characteristics of Demons

Watching too many movies about demon-possession has given some people crazy ideas about what demons are like. It is time to wipe the slate clean and establish a clear, biblical picture of demons. Knowing your enemy is more than half of the battle.

Devil, Demons, Evil Spirits, Unclean Spirits

To start with, we need to make a clear distinction between the devil (singular) and demons (plural). There is only one devil, and he is Satan. People mistakenly refer to "devils"—often picking the usage up from the mistranslation of the word in many versions of the Bible. The Greek word for "devil" is *diabolos*, which means "slanderous" or "slanderer," and it should be used only as a name for Satan himself.

There is one devil, but there are legions of demons. The Greek word for demon (often plural) is *daimon* or *daimonion*. Demons are also known as "evil spirits" or "unclean spirits."[1]

What Does "Demon-Possessed" Mean?

Mistranslation and misusage has created another problem by introducing the term "demon-possessed," which should imply that someone is possessed *with* a demon or demons rather than what it has come to mean—that a person has been taken over by a demon or demons. If you own a jacket, you are possessed *of* or *with* a jacket; you are not possessed *by* your jacket. If you as a believer have a demon, you are possessed of a demon, but the demon does not possess you, even if its influence is considerable.

Possession shows ownership, but someone cannot be owned or possessed by more than one entity. In the case of a believer, that person is possessed by God's Spirit—although the person can also possess (or have) a demon and be heavily under its influence (I don't know why a Christian would want one, but he can certainly have one). The actual Greek usage makes this clear. In biblical terms, a person can *have* an unclean spirit,[2] a person can be *in* or *under the influence of* an unclean spirit that is *upon* him or her[3] and a person can be *demonized*.[4]

You can have something *in* or *on* you without being possessed by it. That is why a believer can be afflicted, harassed, tormented or tainted by a demon without being possessed outright. Think of a house: If you are a born-again believer in Jesus, God has the title deed of your house. But that does not mean that all of the rooms of the house have been cleaned up. Also, that does not mean that you might not sometimes have unwelcome intruders in the house. If you allow Him to do so, the true Owner will help you clean the place up so that He can move into every room.

Demonic Personality Basics

Individual demons have *wills*. How do we know this? By reading scriptural passages such as Matthew 12:44, a passage about the evil spirit that has been cast out of a poorly guarded person: "Then it says, 'I *will* return to my house from which I came'" (NASB, emphasis added). Remember also the story of the legion of demons being sent into the pigs (Mark 5:11–13). In various translations of verse 12, the demons exhibited their strong desire or *will* when they "begged," "implored" and "besought" Jesus for permission to enter the pigs.

That verse also helps to demonstrate that demons have *emotions*—fear and desperation. Another example of demonic emotions can be found in James 2:19, "You believe that God is one; you do well. So do the demons believe and shudder [in terror and horror such as make a man's hair stand on end and contract the surface of his skin]!" (AMP). We can assume that demons do not enjoy positive emotions such as joy, unless it is overlaid with wickedness, such as in wicked glee.

Demons have *knowledge* about the environment around them. They are not omniscient (all-knowing), omnipresent (all-present) or omnipotent (all-powerful) like God. But they do have a partial range of supernatural knowledge that surpasses human knowledge, and sometimes they blurt it out, as they did when Jesus went into the synagogue at Capernaum: "A man in their synagogue who was possessed by an evil spirit cried out, 'What do you want with us, Jesus of Nazareth? Have you come to destroy us? I know who you are—the Holy One of God!'" (Mark 1:23–24, NIV). You see, sometimes demons know more than church people! Another example of demonic knowledge is what happened when the sons of Sceva tried unsuccessfully to cast out demons in Jesus' name. One demon (using the vocal cords of the demonized person, as evil spirits do), said, "Jesus I know, and Paul I know about, but who are you?" (Acts 19:15, AMP).

In addition to having a knowledge or awareness of things outside themselves, demons also have *self-awareness*. They know how they fit into the demonic power hierarchy and they possess strong self-protective instincts. We can see this in the comment that the demon made through the Gerasene demoniac, when he revealed that he was not operating alone (see Mark 5:9). The chief spokesman-demon was aware of His authority over the legion of lesser demons, and he was certainly aware that he had met up with One who possessed more authority than he did.

Demons also have the *ability to speak*, apparently in whatever language is necessary in order to be understood by humans. We noted the verbal responses to Jesus and to the sons of Sceva. It seems that sometimes they take temporary control of the vocal cords of a demonized person. Other times, it seems that the mind of the person is so barraged with demonic input that he or she gives utterance to the deceptive ideas.

One thing that demons do not have is corporeal bodies. They are homeless spirits, and they need to "borrow" the use of human or animal bodies or possessions. They have a *strong desire for a body*. In the story of the Gerasene demoniac, the fact that Jesus cast the demons out of the man and into the pigs is ironic—yes, a herd of pigs will work to house a legion of demons, but to the Jews, pigs are unclean. So Jesus was sending the demons into what was considered an unclean house. Then the pigs went berserk and plunged off the cliff to their deaths, rendering the spirits homeless anyway.

Throughout this book, I have emphasized the importance of personal character and righteousness in preparing to cast out evil spirits as well as keeping them out. If you try to cast out a demon before you crucify the flesh, the demon will be able to find his way back before you know it. I compare it to pulling taffy; it can be very sticky business. Some people try to cast out demons before they take care of the fleshly "garbage" that attracted them in the first place. This will not work very well.

You can (and should) cast out demons whenever you encounter them. But you cannot eradicate them or kill them. The only thing you can (and should) kill is your own flesh. You should crucify it, in fact (see Romans 8:13; 2 Corinthians 4:11).

The Activity of Demonic Spirits

Demons do not seem to take it easy. Because of their degree of knowledge, they understand that they have only a finite amount of time in which to operate. They know that someday they will no longer have authority to roam the earth and harass people. Therefore, they are in a hurry, striving to get as much evil done as quickly as possible.

The undertakings and endeavors of demons all have the same goal—to interfere with the Kingdom of God. Here are their typical activities:

1. Demons *entice* (see James 1:14). When you feel drawn, wooed, seduced, coerced or tempted, you can be sure that you are experiencing the work of evil spirits. This is far different from the guiding or nudging of the Holy Spirit.
2. Demons *deceive* (see 1 Timothy 4:1–2). They try to influence people to make bad decisions. Starting with a bit of the truth, they exaggerate a problem and blow it out of proportion. Their goal is to move people away from solid faith, grace, purity and obedience. To reinforce their efforts, they make use of people whose consciences have been "seared" and hardened over (see 1 Timothy 4:2).
3. Demons *enslave* (see Romans 8:15; 2 Timothy 2:26). Evil spirits chain people up, trapping them and holding them captive. They make people into their puppets, to one degree or another.

4. Demons *torment*. Unclean spirits torment people by stirring up anxiety and inordinate fears, sometimes to the point that people cannot function normally. Relief from torment comes from God: "For God did not give us a spirit of timidity (of cowardice, of craven and cringing and fawning fear), but [He has given us a spirit] of power and of love and of calm and well-balanced mind and discipline and self-control" (2 Timothy 1:7, AMP; see also 1 John 4:18).

5. Demons *drive* and *compel* (see Luke 8:29). Using irrational fears and pressure, evil spirits will force people to do things. The man who was infested with Legion was often driven into the desert. People become addicted to substances or behaviors, feeling compelled to repeat their behavior over and over. They have no control.

6. Demons *defile* (see Titus 1:15). Demons defile people through sin patterns and also through close association with the darkness.

7. Demons *teach*. "The [Holy] Spirit distinctly and expressly declares that in latter times some will turn away from the faith, giving attention to deluding and seducing spirits and doctrines that demons teach" (1 Timothy 4:1, AMP). The Mormons provide a good example of this, because the angel Moroni is not an angel from God; the doctrines taught by Moroni come from the devil. People can become defiled by the darkness and falsehood that comes from the *Book of Mormon*—or from Freemasonry rites or a Unitarian sermon. By such means, demons are teaching falsehood.

8. Demons make people *sick* and *infirm*. "There was a woman there who for eighteen years had had an infirmity caused by a spirit (a demon of sickness). She was bent completely forward and utterly unable to straighten herself up or to

look upward" (Luke 13:11, AMP). The Greek word for "infirmity" means weakness. Evil spirits can create specific physiological, psychological and emotional weaknesses. Every kind of weakness is not necessarily caused by a demon, but some of them are.

9. Demons, therefore, *fight against peace* and *produce restlessness*. Using the tactics at their disposal, they disrupt inner, personal harmony and peace of mind; they interfere with physical well-being; they obstruct harmonious relationships with other people; they interrupt harmonious adjustments to external circumstances.

Does any of this sound familiar to you? How have you experienced firsthand the activity of evil spirits in your life?

For the most part, God will not resist the devil for you, although He will help you to resist when demons come at you from the outside. In their epistles, James and Peter urge believers to resist the enemy: "Submit yourselves therefore to God. Resist the devil, and he will flee from you" (James 4:7, KJV; see also 1 Peter 5:8–9).

When they have come from the outside to the inside, infiltrating a person or an environment, you need to expel them. Do take time to learn what you will need to know beforehand, but do not just hope and wait for somebody else to do it. When you submit to God, your authority gets actualized. You become a terrorist—as far as demons are concerned. You can be a Holy Ghost terrorist, like me. The choice is yours!

Then when demons invade a person or a locale, you can cast them out or expel them. Jesus spent much of His time doing just that: "He went into their synagogues throughout all Galilee, preaching and casting out the demons" (Mark 1:39, NASB; see also Matthew 8:16).

The "Walled City Principle"

You see, you are not supposed to be a victim of your circumstances. Once you invite the Holy Spirit to live inside you, you have the authority to tackle whatever comes against you. Because of His Spirit, you have control over your own human spirit. This gives you divine oversight in every category of your life.

Each person's life is like a walled city. We are supposed to have moral "walls" of protection around our beings. Many times, however, we have only partial walls of protection. The enemy does case studies on us, looking to find breaches in our walls or our gates. When he finds one, he exploits it.

That is why our righteous character matters so much, and it is why we need to guard and watch at all times. "Like a city that is broken into and without walls is a man who has no control over his spirit" (Proverbs 25:28, NASB; see also Proverbs 16:32).

Our "city within" can have many occupants who live in various sectors:

1. *Emotions, attitudes, relationships*: anger, fear, resentment, hatred, rebellion, pride, contention, rejection, death, suicide and more.
2. *Thoughts, the realm of the mind*: doubt, unbelief, indecision, procrastination, compromise, confusion and more.
3. *The tongue*: lying, unclean talk, gossip, blasphemy and more.
4. *Sex*: lust, adultery, pornography, perversion, homosexuality, fantasy, compulsive masturbation and more.
5. *Addictions and habitual responses to frustrations*: gluttony, alcoholism, nicotine addiction, caffeine addiction, drug addiction and more.
6. *Physical infirmities*: allergies, tumors, fits, cramps, heart attacks, arthritis and more.

In the book of Isaiah, the walls of a figurative city are called "Salvation" and its gates are called "Praise" (see Isaiah 60:18). This is a good picture of our own salvation-walled selves. No demons will come through a gate of Praise, because a faith-filled, thankful heart repels them. But if you employ your heart and tongue in the opposite of praise and thanksgiving, immediately you create a breach for enemy access.

This principle applies to the geographical region or location to which God has assigned you. Do not speak negatively about your assigned spot in the Kingdom ("I don't like this place. This is the darkest community, filled with all kinds of immorality," etc.). If your critical heart makes you forget to bless it, pray for it, forgive sinners and demonstrate God's mercy, you have reinforced the darkness and opened the gate to enemy incursion, proclaiming that they are welcome—after all, this must be their kind of place!

Demons are not omnipresent, as I noted earlier. So sometimes you can get away with relaxing your guard. Then, when a breach in your wall does not result in an immediate attack, you may decide that the threat from the "roaring lion" (see 1 Peter 5:8) is not as great as you had thought. But it is. Stay on guard at all times, and remember that one of your best forms of protection is simply your Spirit-filled righteousness.

Scriptural Names of Demonic Spirits

Knowing the name of something helps you to talk about it, teach others about it and address issues related to it. If you want to buy a tool but all you can call it is a "thingy" or a "whatchama-callit," you won't get very far at the hardware store.

In a similar way, simply knowing the name of an entity helps you to deal with it appropriately. Just as people and angels are known by names and nicknames based on behavior or function, so often are evil spirits. Here is a partial list of some of the specific names of demonic beings that I have found mentioned in the Bible:

1. Spirit of infirmity (see Luke 13:11. Note that not all infirmities are caused by demons).
2. Deaf and dumb spirit (see Mark 9:25. Not only can this spirit afflict people with physical deafness and muteness, but it can also hinder people from hearing spiritual truth, putting invisible earmuffs on them and keeping them spiritually ignorant).
3. Unclean spirit (used more than twenty times in the New Testament. See, for example, Matthew 12:43; Mark 1:23; Luke 11:24).
4. Spirit of blindness (see Matthew 12:22).
5. Familiar spirit (see Leviticus 20:27; Isaiah 8:19; 2 Kings 23:24). To deceive and mislead, this spirit impersonates someone who is familiar to you.
6. Angel of light (see 2 Corinthians 11:14). This is one of the disguises of Satan.
7. Lying spirit (see 1 Kings 22:22–23; 2 Chronicles 18:20, 22).
8. Seducing spirit (see 1 Timothy 4:1).
9. Foul spirit (see Mark 9:25; Revelation 18:2).
10. Jealous spirit (see Numbers 5:14, 30).
11. Spirit of divination (see Acts 16:16).
12. Spirit of fear (see 2 Timothy 1:7; 1 John 4:18).
13. Spirit of heaviness (see Isaiah 61:3).

Sometimes it is difficult to tell if something like a "spirit of heaviness" is an actual demon or merely a heavy environment or a depressed mood. However, your response to either should be similar: (1) Check for breaches in the wall and remedy them; (2) stir up your love for God and your faith in Him; and (3) cast out what seems to be an intruder.

What to Watch Out For

How can an unclean spirit bring a person into bondage? In as many ways as there are individual people and spirits—but most of the ways fall into identifiable patterns.

Spirits of Lust or Adultery

Someone who makes a habit of viewing sexually immoral movies or television shows, or who chooses pornographic magazines or websites, opens the "eye gate" of his or her walled city and makes it easy for evil spirits to come in.

Spirits of Fear or Suicide

Death-dealing spirits may enter due to occult practices or family curses. Some may come in because of sudden shock, such as when an angry parent gives a child a very harsh verbal scolding or abandons the child as a means of discipline.

Occult Spirits

Activities such as séances, playing with Ouija boards or engaging in other occult practices can open the door to occult spirits. Sometimes the presence of occult spirits will be reinforced by nightmares, hearing noises, hearing voices or seeing images.

Addictions or Gluttony

Partaking improperly of food, alcohol, nicotine or drugs can invite spirits of addiction or gluttony to enter and dwell within.

Spirit of Death

Self-imposed curses or death wishes ("I wish I were dead"), occult involvement and generational curses all serve as invitations for a spirit of death.

Spirit of Rejection

Again, self-imposed curses or vows ("I wish I were never born"; "I am going to get along without people") can provide an open door for a spirit of rejection. Such strong emotional verbalizations can give the enemy a foothold.

In later chapters, we will discuss some of these in more detail.

What to Expect

Of the religious leaders, the prophet Jeremiah said, "They have also healed the hurt of My people slightly, saying, 'Peace, peace!' when there is no peace" (Jeremiah 6:14; see also Jeremiah 8:11). Deep wounds had been covered but not cleansed. One of the reasons that the wounds of God's people are not yet healed is because often the Church has turned a blind eye to the work of evil spirits.

We must employ "probes" and "forceps" to expose and extract evil spirits. Otherwise, the wounds of God's people will continue to fester. Evil spirits must be recognized and driven out. To minister to human needs without discerning evil spirits and dealing with them is like "beating the air" instead of fighting (see 1 Corinthians 9:26).

Jesus set the example for us. A quarter to a third of His ministry time was spent on deliverance. If that was true of Him when He walked the earth, how much more should it be true of His Body, the Church, today? Deliverance should be our work as much as it was His, because He works through us now. It is true that "whoever calls on the name of the LORD will be delivered" (Joel 2:32, NASB; see also Acts 2:21).

PART II

Revealing and Defeating the Enemy's Plans

4

Truths and Tactics of Temptation

We have a "Trojan Horse" problem. At some point in time, individually and collectively, we have opened the door and welcomed something that appeared to be good, only to find out later that we had received an enemy into our precincts. This could have happened when we were unenlightened, before we were in Christ. It could have happened through our patterns of unrepented sin. However it happened, it did happen, and now we have a problem.

As soon as the enemy drops his disguise, we realize that we have an intruder on the premises. Now we have a double problem—we not only have to evict him, we also have to clean the place up and rebuild our walls of salvation to keep him on the outside.

One of the best ways to keep the enemy out is to learn about how temptation works; in particular, what makes us vulnerable, and how we can better resist it.

Foundational Truths about Temptation

Many of us stumble in the gray area between temptation that comes from the enemy and the testing that comes from God. We do not understand the difference, if any, between them.

One foundational truth about temptation is this: *God tests but He never tempts* (see James 1:13). The purpose of testing sent from Him is to strengthen us and to sanctify us; Jesus came to give life more abundantly. On the other side, the purpose of satanic temptation is to deceive, kill, steal and destroy (see John 10:10). God's testing sets us apart as His own children. Satan's tempting separates us from God.

Satan does not have to come up with original ideas with which to tempt people because people come up with plenty of ideas on their own. *All temptation originates in the flesh*, as we learn from the well-known passage in the first chapter of James:

> Let no one say when he is tempted, "I am tempted by God"; for God cannot be tempted by evil, nor does He Himself tempt anyone. But each one is tempted when he is drawn away by his own desires and enticed. Then, when desire has conceived, it gives birth to sin; and sin, when it is full-grown, brings forth death.
>
> James 1:13–15

Our flesh sets fire to sin. Satan simply fans the flame.

We must be clear about this: *Temptation itself is not sin.* Jesus was tempted repeatedly, but He remained sinless (see Hebrews 2:17–18; 4:15). Temptation is not sin; it is merely part of the human condition. Naturally, the enemy tries to persuade people otherwise, making them feel guilty for having had a temptation, even if they resisted it successfully. Martin Luther is quoted as having said, "You can't prevent the birds from flying over your head, but you can keep them from building a nest in your hair." Martin Lloyd-Jones, longtime pastor of Westminster Chapel in London, was known for emphasizing that a temptation only becomes sin when we accept it, when we fondle it, when we enjoy it.

So temptation itself is not a blot on your righteousness. It only proves that you are human. God made you with appetites, desires and the ability to feel. The essence and strength of temptation consists of a twofold enticement: (1) *satisfying legitimate needs through illegitimate means* and (2) *pushing virtue to extreme religious legalism* (which comes from a performance-based desire for acceptance).

Jesus' wilderness temptations provide an example of the former. Here is how Sam Storms describes it:

> Bread is not evil. Neither is the desire to alleviate hunger by eating it, especially after you've fasted for forty days! Divine protection is a valid promise in Scripture (Psalm 91). Authority over the kingdoms of the world is something God promised the Son long ago (cf. Psalm 2). The temptation, therefore, was aimed at seducing Jesus into achieving divinely approved ends by sinful and illegitimate means.[1]

A final foundational truth about temptation is this: *The more often you say yes to a temptation, the more difficult it becomes to say no.* Sin is addictive. It is habit-forming, building to ever-increasing dimensions. Because sin has a lie at the core of it, it offers one thing and produces another, steadily hardening a person's soul over time (see Hebrews 3:12–13). Sin almost always feels good, which serves to cover the end result—death. Death to your heart. Death to your emotions. Death to your soul. Death to relationships. Sin will tell you a partial truth—which is the same as a lie—and the more often you fall for it, the harder it becomes to resist.

The Tactics of Temptation

The devil especially likes to tempt people when their faith is fresh and vulnerable. This comes with the territory. A recently converted Christian is an irresistible target for Satan (see 1 Timothy 3:6).

He also tempts people when their faith is strong—or so they think. When people feel invulnerable to sin, they tend to slip into living by their own strength, and it becomes easy for Satan to get his hooks into them.

Temptation lurks when people are in an environment that is new or strange to them. I travel a lot, and I try to stay alert to this one. At home, I am attuned to the spiritual atmosphere and I have learned to resist certain things. When I go to a new place, the demonic assignments are different and at first I am culturally unaware of the enemy's schemes. Suddenly, I am being tempted with something I had not thought about for twenty years.

From time to time, each one of us will be tested with afflictions—physical, mental, emotional and spiritual (see Matthew 4:1–11; Job 2:1–10). Even Jesus was not exempt. The test will attract some unwelcome temptation, because the enemy is not blind to what is going on. Paul advised people to not be ignorant of the devil's schemes (see 2 Corinthians 2:11). While you are being tested by fire, the enemy will come along to tempt you, whispering, "Why don't you just quit? Give up. Nobody's watching. What difference does it make?" and so forth.

Satan will also send temptations your way when you are *not* being tested, when you have just conquered a spiritual mountain and you feel great. Heed the lesson of Elijah in 1 Kings 18 and 19. He had achieved a spectacular victory over the prophets of Baal, and the next thing you know he wanted to die. He ran away, hid in the wilderness and became so depressed and confused that God had to send in an angelic rescue squad.

Perhaps Satan's more effective tactic is tempting us to put his thoughts into our minds and then blaming us for having them (see 1 Chronicles 21:1; Matthew 16:13–23; John 13:2; Acts 5:1–3). We mistake his thoughts for our thoughts, because so often he speaks in the first person. He says, for instance, "I feel bad today. I feel cut off from God." This is the truth—he *does* feel bad and cut off from God. But the person into whose mind he has planted his thoughts assumes that those negative thoughts are his or hers. I found advice about this tactic of temptation in an old book called *The Christian in Complete Armour* by William Gurnall:

> When thoughts or inclinations contrary to the will and ways of God creep in, many dear Christians mistake these miserable orphans for their own children, and take upon themselves the full responsibility for these carnal passions. So deftly does the devil slip his own thoughts into the saints' bosoms that by the time they begin to whimper, he is already out of sight. And the misbegotten notions are his own. So he bears the shame himself, and Satan has accomplished his purposes.[2]

A related tactic is for Satan to launch his accusations as if they were from the Holy Spirit. How can we distinguish between satanic accusation and divine conviction? By their fruit—the devil's accusation releases discouragement, shame and hopeless condemnation, whereas God's conviction brings godly sorrow, which unlocks repentance and hope and freedom.

When License Becomes Licentiousness

You and I will rarely be tempted to commit obvious sins such as murder, robbery or rape. The enemy realizes that we will recognize them as flagrant sins and refuse to act on them.

Instead, his tactic is to entice us to push the limits of something until it becomes sin. It starts out as something good, or at least neutral. The devil treats us like the proverbial frog on the stove as he gradually turns up the heat under us, hoping that we will not notice that we are getting closer to death as we yield to incremental temptations. Here (with acknowledgment to Neil Anderson in *The Bondage Breaker*[3]) are a number of statements that reveal the sinful results of stretching the limits:

- Need for physical rest becomes laziness.
- Quietness becomes non-communicativeness.
- The ability to turn a profit becomes greed.
- Enjoyment of the pleasures of life becomes intemperance.
- The gift of physical pleasure becomes sensuality.
- A healthy interest in the possessions of others becomes covetousness.
- Enjoyment of eating becomes gluttony.
- A sense of personal responsibility becomes selfishness.
- Self-respect becomes pride.
- Factual communication becomes gossip.
- Realistic caution becomes unbelief.
- Optimism becomes insensitivity to people's current needs.
- Anger becomes rage and ill-temperedness.
- Care for others becomes over-protectiveness.
- Judgment becomes condemnation.
- Same-sex friendships become tainted with homosexuality.
- Sexual liberty becomes immorality.
- Conscientiousness becomes perfectionism.
- Generosity becomes profligacy.
- Carefulness becomes anxiety and fear.
- Spiritual compatibility becomes illegal soul ties. (Be careful of those compatibility tests you can take online.)

- Freedom becomes an occasion for the flesh.
- Encouragement becomes flattery.
- Pursuit of goals becomes a driving compulsion.
- Prophetic words become a replacement for the written Word (i.e., you are more impressed with the words coming out of you than you are with the Word coming into you).
- Success motivation becomes boastful "pride of life."
- An emotional healing ministry is converted into a "rescuer" mentality.
- A healing touch becomes over-familiar and inappropriate.

I am sure that you could add to this list from your personal experience. Make it a practice to evaluate your motivations regularly. Learn to detect the shifting sand underfoot and learn to plant your feet on the solid Rock of Jesus Christ.

Tactics for Resisting Temptation

Satan's goal is always the same—to deceive you into believing that whatever he is tempting you to do is as harmless as it seems and that yielding to his temptation will bring you pleasure (with no repercussions). He never gets tired of tempting people. Therefore, we need to be prepared to resist his tactics.

What tactics of your own should you have ready? Here are eight basic ones:

1. First and foremost—know yourself. Know your weak points, which is where the devil will attack you most often. My friend Bill puts it this way: "Ask yourself this question. If I were the devil, how would I attack me?" Get real about your points of vulnerability. Get help if you need to.

2. If you cannot eliminate the temptation in the first place, then deal with it as quickly as possible. At the beginning of a temptation—not at the end of it—confront it, so that you can conquer it more easily. Never wait until the temptation has worn you down.
3. Pray preventive prayers (see Matthew 6:13). "An ounce of prevention is worth a pound of cure."
4. Pray protective prayers (see Matthew 26:41). Keep the walls of your "city" strong (see Proverbs 16:32; 25:28).
5. Flee. Simply flee. You don't have to stick around to see how close to the edge you can get without falling (see 1 Corinthians 6:18; 10:14; 1 Timothy 6:11; 2 Timothy 2:22). Turn around before you get into the checkout line. Walk out of the movie. Close your eyes when you glimpse something that tantalizes you.
6. Use your Bible. Jesus did (see Matthew 4 and Luke 4). Make use of the sword of the Spirit.
7. Resist. Don't give way. Sometimes that's all it takes. "Resist the devil, and he will flee from you" (James 4:7, KJV).
8. Make yourself accountable to others. Not only do I have a board of directors for my ministry, I also have a three-man personal advisory team and they hold me accountable. "Therefore confess your sins to each other and pray for each other so that you may be healed. The prayer of a righteous man is powerful and effective" (James 5:16, NIV).

You have to prepare for temptation, because it will surely come. And when it comes, it will be . . . *tempting.* In other words, you will *want* to entertain those tempting thoughts. You will never be tempted to eat foods you do not like. You will never be tempted sexually by members of the opposite sex who are repulsive-looking. You will never be tempted to bend the truth in order to obtain a promotion you do not desire.

You will be tempted to do something that appears to be satisfying. With the temptation before your eyes, you will forget about obedience, just as Adam and Eve did. The devil will tempt you through one of the three age-old channels of temptation:

- The lust of the flesh. Lust does not refer only to sex. Any kind of craving that appeals to your physical senses is lust of the flesh.
- The lust of the eyes. You covet something, and you throw aside prudence and obedience in order to get it.
- The pride of life. Angling for the spotlight, you promote yourself and exalt your reputation.

In His wisdom, John capsulated these three channels of temptation when he wrote, "For all that is in the world—the lust of the flesh, the lust of the eyes, and the pride of life—is not of the Father but is of the world. And the world is passing away, and the lust of it; but he who does the will of God abides forever" (1 John 2:16–17).

Feed Yourself the Right Things

Do not think for a minute that sin will satisfy you better than God. As a matter of fact, you never can satisfy the desires of the flesh without Him. Jesus said, "Blessed are those who hunger and thirst for righteousness, for they shall be satisfied" (Matthew 5:6, NASB).

Feed yourself the right things, all of which come straight from the Father. Right relationships, living in the power of the Holy Spirit and right fruit of the Spirit—those are the things that will satisfy you, body, soul and spirit. A life that is lived in the Kingdom of God, where righteousness, peace and joy rule and reign is far better than any kind of one-night-stand satisfaction.

Do not stop short. After you starve out evil intruders, fill the void with God's nourishing, abundant life. Only in Him will you find the pleasures that are greater than any tempter can offer.

5

Battle Plans for Overcomers

You have to run over the devil before he runs over you. You are standing on a battlefield (a different one from the one you were standing on last year at this time). You may be standing in the middle of an army, or you may be standing all alone.

Are you just going to stand there, waiting to see what will happen? Or are you going to do something that will allow you to get and keep the upper hand?

King David gave us a psalm that we should graft onto ourselves so that we can be true overcomers: "I pursued my enemies and overtook them; I did not turn back till they were destroyed" (Psalm 18:37, NIV). Earlier in the same psalm, he expressed his utter dependency on God when his enemies proved to be too strong for him: "He rescued me from my powerful enemy, from my foes, who were too strong for me. They confronted me in the day of my disaster, but the LORD was my support" (Psalm 18:17–18, NIV).

He was a true overcomer—determined to make an end of his enemies, but always aware that he needed help doing it.

The Book of Wars

In the book of Numbers, I found this interesting phrase: "Therefore it is said in the Book of the Wars of the LORD. . ." (Numbers 21:14). What is this book? The Book of the Wars of the Lord is not part of the canon of Scripture, nor are several other books that are mentioned in the Bible, such as the book of remembrance (see Malachi 3:16) or the book of tears (see Psalm 56:8). Perhaps we can construe the Book of the Wars of the Lord to be a book that has not yet been finished—and that we ourselves can help to complete as we engage the enemy, one skirmish at a time.

For each of us, the combat will not be over until the day we die. Born in the midst of battle and born for battle, we are following our Commander-in-Chief, whose mission was to destroy the works of the devil. We are not warring against our spouses, our children, our bosses or our pastors (even if some of the time it seems like it). We are battling against besetting spiritual forces of wickedness.

I like to think that our ongoing struggle is a sign of life, and proof that we have not yet been conquered. The Lord of Life is waging warfare through us. Our efforts are—or should be—springing from the placement of the Son of God in our personal lives. How central is He in your life, your family, your lineage, your congregation, your ministry, your city, your nation? How much of His Kingdom has come? How much of His will has been done?

If you haven't already realized it, now is the time to see that the battle is not about you; it is about *Him*. He is the driving force behind every spiritual battle, as He retrieves and redeems and restores. Transforming the redeemed ones as He leads them forward on every battlefield, He is making sure that the entire Church, His Bride, will be beautiful for Him.

As we engage in struggle after struggle, not only are we sub-jugating Satan, we are also being transformed, individually and as a body. The whole Church is in metamorphosis, becoming a new creation in Christ, growing and maturing and overcoming the darkness of the old regime.[1]

War Scriptures

Battle fatigue often hits in the midst of the fiercest fighting, but the Lord will always revive, restore and return us to life. Scriptural reassurances abound:

> When you pass through the waters,
>   I will be with you;
> and when you pass through the rivers,
>   they will not sweep over you.
> When you walk through the fire,
>   you will not be burned;
>   the flames will not set you ablaze.
>
> Isaiah 43:2, NIV

> Though I walk in the midst of trouble, You will revive
>   me;
>   You will stretch forth Your hand against the wrath of
>   my enemies,
>   And Your right hand will save me.
> The LORD will accomplish what concerns me;
>   Your lovingkindness, O LORD, is everlasting;
>   Do not forsake the works of Your hands.
>
> Psalm 138:7–8, NASB

Did you notice where He revives you? *In the midst of trouble.* Such a simple statement—such a profound truth. Light shines brightest in darkness. Are you in trouble right now? Do not quit. Never give up. Take hold of your shield of enduring faith and wage war alongside your brothers and sisters.

Remember that you are fighting an unseen enemy who is behind all of the opposition that you can see and feel (see Ephesians 6:12). You have the authority of the One who called you, who said:

> I saw Satan falling like a lightning [flash] from heaven.
> Behold! I have given you authority and power to trample upon serpents and scorpions, and [physical and mental strength and ability] over all the power that the enemy [possesses]; and nothing shall in any way harm you.
> Nevertheless, do not rejoice at this, that the spirits are subject to you, but rejoice that your names are enrolled in heaven.
>
> Luke 10:18–20, AMP

The Body of Jesus Christ tramples on every enemy, enforcing the victory of Calvary. This battle is part of our birthright. However, as the Lord said, we are not supposed to rejoice merely because evil spirits must leave when we say so, but because we are being prepared for a heavenly destination. He wants us to have His perspective.

He wants us to remember that, although we will have to suffer the sting of the enemy's wrath (as He Himself did) it will not last forever. We can be glad about that! "For this reason, rejoice, O heavens and you who dwell in them. Woe to the earth and the sea, because the devil has come down to you, having great wrath, knowing that he has only a short time" (Revelation 12:12, NASB).

The devil and his minions are filled with terror. Although they are not omniscient, omnipotent or omni-anything, they do know that their time is short, and this knowledge increases their wrath. They are trying to wreak as much carnage as possible before the final curtain goes down. This can help us as soldiers in God's army. We can adopt an attitude that says, "Dude, you may have inflicted some wounds on me, but you do not have the final word. I've seen the end of the book, and I know you will lose."

Every skirmish has the same ultimate outcome—victory. For "no temptation has seized you except what is common to man. And God is faithful; he will not let you be tempted beyond what you can bear. But when you are tempted, he will also provide a way out so that you can stand up under it" (1 Corinthians 10:13, NIV).

Why Is Satan Picking on You?

Do you sometimes feel as if the enemy has painted a bull's-eye on you? What did you do to attract his unwelcome attention?

Well, for one thing, you are God's friend. God created you for His pleasure and He takes pleasure in you (see Revelation 4:11). He takes so much pleasure in you that He sent His Son to redeem you from the hand of His enemy so that He could adopt you as His child. He takes so much pleasure in you that He is beautifying you and making you able to reflect His image the way you were created to do.

And since Satan cannot assault God directly, he attacks God's friends. He tries to undermine the ground beneath your feet. He tries to make you deny your Lord. The devil tries to paralyze your planning, abort your dreams and dilute your hope. He opposes everything that could help you stay close to God's heart.

The truth of the situation is that the devil is mighty jealous of you. Who do you think you are, giving glory to God, surrendering yourself to Him as your Father and Lord—and resisting evil at every turn?

What Are Satan's Favorite Tactics?

Satan is not particularly creative. He exercises his malice in certain predictable (and, therefore, resistible) ways. With his limited repertoire, all he can do is to mix standard ingredients into variations on the same recipe. Here is a quick list of his favorite tactics against human beings:

1. Delay. To weaken you and wear you out. To make you lose your way (see Daniel 10:2–14).
2. Deceit. To derail God's purposes by making spiritual principles into legalism. To move you from the stability of truth to the instability of error (see Revelation 12:9).
3. Distraction. To break your focus. To make you concentrate on a side issue. A time of great intimacy with God can turn into a time of great battle (see Proverbs 4:27).
4. Disappointment. To magnify the weaknesses of others; to offend you and to embitter you.

Delay, deceit, distraction and disappointment—each one of these tactics is slow-acting. You may not recognize them at first. Sometimes it seems that Satan is more patient than you are as he encroaches on your peace, inch by inch. He cannot derail you instantly, although it may seem abrupt when it happens.

To detect evil encroachment more quickly, assess your life experiences to become aware of your personal Achilles' heel, your point of greatest vulnerability. Some people's greatest weakness is unbelief. For others it is bitterness or revenge. For others it is checking out, backing off, quitting. Everybody is different. One person may be vulnerable because of a time of grief or fatigue. Others may be prone to volcanic anger. Ask the Lord to show you your greatest weakness, because that is where your enemy will concentrate his efforts.

Realize, however, that once you shore up your defenses in your area of greatest weakness, some other area will become vulnerable, and the enemy will circle around again. He's stalking you, just waiting for you to stumble.

When Does Satan Hit the Hardest?

The devil works in cycles. He attacks and pulls back. He hits you and then he shifts around to the other side. This could be disorienting (and he wants it to be), but you can anticipate his moves. You can predict the seasons of your attack.

You will remember what happened to Jesus at the end of His time of temptation in the wilderness. After He had overcome every temptation, "Then the devil left him, and angels came and attended him" (Matthew 4:11, NIV). In other words, the forty-day attack was over with. There would be more battles later, in another season. The enemy would regroup. Taking advantage of the breather, angels helped Jesus to regroup as well.

We can observe this same pattern of attacking and regrouping in our own lives. The two reasons why Satan pulls back are: (1) because you won, and he has to go off to lick his wounds, or (2) he wants to trick you and put you off your balance so you will let your guard down. Either way, you need to be ready for the next round.

One of the best ways to prepare in anticipation is to assess your own seasonal cycle of weakness. This is reminiscent of spiritual mapping, personal spiritual mapping. Look over the literal seasons of your life. When do you tend to struggle with depression? In the winter? When have you been hit with lust? In the heat of summer, on the beach? Gear up for that season beforehand. Keep the sword of the Spirit at your side, keep prayer-watching, steer clear of sin. Do not think for a minute that just because you are not under attack right now, you are free and clear. Keep an eye on yourself and keep an eye out for the enemy. Make your next battle a decisive victory.

Some of Satan's greatest attacks will probably happen when you get too little sleep (and I would like to tell that to every college student I know). We are all more vulnerable when we are tired. When you have worked yourself to the bone, you are weak not only because of physical fatigue, but also because of emotional and mental fatigue. As I write this book, I have temporarily been weakened by fatigue and grief due to the loss of my dear wife. The Lord has told me that one of my most effective tactics against temptation and discouragement right now is simply rest. As I make time for physical rest, I make it a point to rest my spirit—in faith. He has also told me to pray more in tongues, so I have been doing that—up to two hours at a time. I firmly believe that resting is not only serving to restore my strength, but also to fend off the enemy's further assaults.

Watch out also when you have major changes in your life, especially geographical relocations. Crisis occurs on the eve of change.

The enemy always tries to thwart the plans of God. Even with his partial knowledge, he knows when someone is destined for greatness (he can hear the prophecies, too). You may not be a Moses or a Jesus with Pharaoh or Herod tracking you with murder in his eyes, but look at what has happened to an entire generation as a result of the legalization of abortion in 1973. God destined this generation for greatness, and the enemy has already mowed down millions of innocent babies before they could emerge into the light of day.

In a similar way, the enemy hits desperately hard when a specific miracle is leaving the hand of God. Daniel is the clearest example of this. For twenty-one days, Daniel fasted and prayed, sweating and trembling and troubled almost beyond endurance (see Daniel 10) before a breakthrough occurred. When you make an effort to take a stand, the degree and intensity of spiritual warfare will be proportional to the territory that you are about to possess. Look at it through a positive lens; all the hell that you have been going through could be a prophetic indication of the great things that are about to happen in your life.

Have you noticed that when you are next in line for a promotion, the enemy tries to stop you? Job is the perfect example. The enemy threw his whole arsenal at Job and he nearly knocked him out of the running, but Job remained true to God through it all. As far as we know, he never had to go through something like that again.

How to Shorten Your Seasons of Struggle

So seasons of struggle will be a "given." Yet you do not need to prolong the agony. Can you shorten your seasons of struggle? I believe you can, and I believe that the Bible is filled with good advice toward this end.

Your Special Weapons

I cannot emphasize enough the power and efficacy of Scripture. As Jesus did in the midst of His wilderness temptation, you must know and speak the Word of God. Not only will the Word put a stop to the enemy's lies, but it will also build you up so that you can stand firm. Here are a couple of words from the Word about the effectiveness of the Word:

> Do your best to present yourself to God as one approved, a workman who does not need to be ashamed and who correctly handles the word of truth.
>
> 2 Timothy 2:15, NIV

> All Scripture is inspired by God and profitable for teaching, for reproof, for correction, for training in righteousness; so that the man of God may be adequate, equipped for every good work.
>
> 2 Timothy 3:16–17, NASB

Let the Holy Spirit and the Word permeate your mind and heart so that your conversations reflect the mentality of a conqueror. This gives new meaning to the proverb, "Death and life are in the power of the tongue, and those who love it will eat its fruit" (Proverbs 18:21).

Always remember the power of the name of the Lord. "The name of the Lord is a strong tower; the [consistently] righteous man [upright and in right standing with God] runs into it and is safe, high [above evil] and strong" (Proverbs 18:10, AMP). Declare His name, loudly or quietly, and expect your enemy to fall back:

> Therefore God also has highly exalted Him and given Him the name which is above every name, that at the name of Jesus every knee should bow, of those in heaven, and of those on earth, and of those under the earth.
>
> Philippians 2:9–10

Do not forget to tap into the power of prayer. "The effective prayer of a righteous man can accomplish much" (James 5:16, NASB). Fasting adds power to your prayers:

> Is this not the fast which I choose,
>   To loosen the bonds of wickedness,
>   To undo the bands of the yoke,
>   And to let the oppressed go free
>   And break every yoke?
>
> Isaiah 58:6, NASB

Get others involved in the praying. Call your believing friends and ask them to pray for you. Never underestimate the extra power of a prayer of agreement:

> I tell you the truth, whatever you bind on earth will be bound in heaven, and whatever you loose on earth will be loosed in heaven.

Again, I tell you that if two of you on earth agree about anything you ask for, it will be done for you by my Father in heaven.

Matthew 18:18–19, NIV

Keep praising God through everything. Not only does praise express and build up your faith, but it also creates a climate that Satan cannot tolerate. What a wonderful weapon for bringing light into darkness! Remember how a few psalms played on a little harp drove the evil spirit away from King Saul: "So it came about whenever the evil spirit from God came to Saul, David would take the harp and play it with his hand; and Saul would be refreshed and be well, and the evil spirit would depart from him" (1 Samuel 16:23, NASB).

Honor the veterans of spiritual battles and learn from their successes and failures. Sometimes you will have "vets" nearby who can mentor you. Other times, you will need to resort to good books and helpful messages from people far away, many of whom will have gone home to their reward years before you were born. "A wise man will hear and increase in learning, and a man of understanding will acquire wise counsel" (Proverbs 1:5, NASB).

Take it from this veteran, you *must* learn when to rest and not directly engage the enemy. The devil's job is to wear down the saints (see Daniel 7:25), and the spirit of the Antichrist comes to do the same (see 1 John 4:3). Therefore, seek wisdom for your warring and learn to rest, both spiritually and physically.

Day after day, clothe yourself by faith with God's spiritual armor: "Therefore put on God's complete armor, that you may be able to resist and stand your ground on the evil day [of danger], and, having done all [the crisis demands], to stand [firmly in your place]" (Ephesians 6:13, AMP).

As you turn the pages of the following chapters, I will be giving you many more tips for countering enemy advances.

6

Exercising Kingdom Authority

Picture this: a kid with a peashooter attacking a fortified castle. That is a little bit what you might be like if you fail to understand the subject of Kingdom authority. For your own safety and for the welfare of the people you love, you need to make sure you have a strong grasp on the truth here. Just what does it mean to exercise "Kingdom authority"? Why bother with it? Where does this authority come from? What can it accomplish? Who can have a share in it? Can it be lost? Can it be regained?

The subject of Kingdom authority is pivotal; everything about spiritual warfare depends on it.

The Enemy's Plan—Overruled by God's Plan

Reviewing the facts, we remember that Satan, in the time before human time, became jealous of God's glory and rebelled. No longer did he want to lead or even participate in the high praises of the God who had created him. In response, God banished him from His presence, casting him out with all of his rebellious under-angels.

Immediately, Satan established a rival spiritual kingdom in opposition to God, ruling over these fallen angels in the heavenly realm and over demonic spirits on earth. For eons since, he has been consumed with gaining as much control of the world's systems as possible and receiving universal worship for himself. His forces, in their relentless effort to rob God of honor and displace the Son from His privileged position, have labored to confuse and harm the people of the earth so that they will be his captives. His objective has always been the same—to keep people from knowing, obeying and honoring God. This is his plan, and he is intent on it.

God, however, has retained the upper hand. He is the One who is all-knowing and all-powerful, and Satan cannot approach His level of superiority. Early on, God launched a concerted response to Satan's rebellion that continues to this day. The centerpiece of the Father's plan is His only Son, Jesus.

The ones who will give allegiance to Him are the ones who will populate the Kingdom of God. They are God's allies in the spiritual warfare that has continued to rage on for centuries after the decisive events of Jesus' life on earth. Although Jesus won the ultimate victory over the powers of darkness through His death and His resurrection and He introduced the Kingdom permanently into the earth realm, He did not want to terminate the spiritual battle until He had reaped as many souls as possible for that Kingdom. As a consequence, far from being over, the spiritual upheaval continues.

That is where we come in. Walking on our piece of the planet, God has invested us with His authority to undertake two special responsibilities: (1) to restrain Satan's forces on earth until God's purposes of grace have been fulfilled, and (2) to participate in the heavenly wrestling match. Sometimes, joining ourselves with other people who have been set free, we can dislodge a territorial spirit over a geographical area, displacing dark angels so that the angels of light can prevail. Walking in spiritual freedom, we can release the Kingdom of God into our present environment, freeing more captives and giving glory to the King. Through us, Jesus Himself still walks the dusty roads, healing and delivering the captives, assembling an army for His Kingdom one soul at a time.

How do we do this? Certainly not on our own strength or in our own wisdom. We do it in faith. On what is our faith based? On the firmly established authority of our righteous Savior, Jesus.

Who Is the Highest?

Without being simplistic, the facts speak for themselves. If you want to be on the winning side, you must surrender your allegiance to all other gods and idols (including the idol of your self) and follow the King. God is the highest authority. He always will be the highest authority because He always has been.

In the first verse of the Bible, we read, "In the beginning God . . ." (Genesis 1:1). It does not say, "In the beginning the devil. . . ." There is no question about who was in authority in heaven. God created both the heavens and the earth and their populations of heavenly and earthly beings—including Satan. Satan did not get there first. He did not create anything. "By faith we understand that the universe was formed at God's command, so that what is seen was not made out of what was visible" (Hebrews 11:3, NIV).

Everything is held together by God's supremacy, and nothing can dislodge Him from His position. He is the beginning and the end, the Alpha and the Omega. As He put it to John: "I am the First and the Last" (Revelation 1:17).

He can delegate His authority to others, and that is what we are going to talk about in this chapter. But it must be delegated, not usurped. Historically, when people try to abrogate His authority, they fail miserably. Satan tried it, and it most definitely did not work. Originally, God had delegated a great deal of authority to the angel of light we know as Lucifer. But that authority was stripped from him when he rebelled, and he will never get a second chance.

Human beings misused their authority, too, following in Satan's footsteps. By the time of Noah, God was so weary of the mess they had caused that He decided to destroy most of the earth He had made in the flood (see Genesis 6–9). Then, after the earth had been repopulated and men decided to promote themselves once again in the form of the tower of Babel, God intervened again, asserting His authority by confusing their language and scattering them (see Genesis 11).

This pattern has repeated itself until the present. Why do people not get the message that the whole world has always been His, and it always will be? "The earth is the Lord's, and the fullness of it, the world and they who dwell in it" (Psalm 24:1, AMP). So although it seems to have been taken over by the enemy, God has never lost possession of it for a moment.

Psalm 104 contains twenty-four assertions of God's sovereign authority and ownership over the earth. Far more than poetic hyperbole, these are statements of fact about God's sovereign authority. For example:

> O LORD my God, You are very great:
>> You are clothed with honor and majesty,
> Who cover Yourself with light as with a garment,
>> Who stretch out the heavens like a curtain.
> He lays the beams of His upper chambers in the waters,
>> Who makes the clouds His chariot,
>> Who walks on the wings of the wind,

Who makes His angels spirits,
　　His ministers a flame of fire.
You who laid the foundations of the earth,
　　So that it should not be moved forever. . . .
O LORD, how manifold are Your works!
　　In wisdom You have made them all.
　　The earth is full of Your possessions—
. . . You send forth Your Spirit, they are created;
　　And You renew the face of the earth.
May the glory of the LORD endure forever.

Psalm 104:1–5, 24, 30–31

So no matter where you are on the earth and no matter what is happening, God is in charge. Everything belongs to Him, even the most evil and immoral environment or the most violent war zones. The more God's people come into alignment with Him and exercise His delegated authority wherever they go, the more He is able to "renew the face of the earth."

Satan, the Fallen

The prophet Ezekiel gave us a picture of the angel who became arrogant enough to challenge the sovereign Lord of the Universe:

You were the seal of perfection,
Full of wisdom and perfect in beauty.
You were in Eden, the garden of God;
Every precious stone was your covering:
The sardius, topaz, and diamond,
Beryl, onyx, and jasper,
Sapphire, turquoise, and emerald with gold.
The workmanship of your timbrels and pipes
Was prepared for you on the day you were created.
You were the anointed cherub who covers;

I established you;
You were on the holy mountain of God;
You walked back and forth in the midst of fiery stones.
You were perfect in your ways from the day you were
    created,
Till iniquity was found in you.
By the abundance of your trading
You became filled with violence within,
And you sinned;
Therefore I cast you as a profane thing
Out of the mountain of God;
And I destroyed you, O covering cherub,
From the midst of the fiery stones.
Your heart was lifted up because of your beauty;
You corrupted your wisdom for the sake of your splendor;
I cast you to the ground,
I laid you before kings,
That they might gaze at you.
You defiled your sanctuaries
By the multitude of your iniquities,
By the iniquity of your trading;
Therefore I brought fire from your midst;
It devoured you,
And I turned you to ashes upon the earth
In the sight of all who saw you.
All who knew you among the peoples are astonished at
    you;
You have become a horror,
And shall be no more forever.

Ezekiel 28:12–19

Before the Fall, this amazingly beautiful being was as bright as the morning star. But as soon as he asserted himself above God, he was cut down swiftly, like a dagger-flash of lightning (see Luke 10:18):

How you are fallen from heaven,
O Lucifer, son of the morning!
How you are cut down to the ground,
You who weakened the nations!
For you have said in your heart:
"I will ascend into heaven,
I will exalt my throne above the stars of God;
I will also sit on the mount of the congregation
On the farthest sides of the north;
I will ascend above the heights of the clouds,
I will be like the Most High."
Yet you shall be brought down to Sheol,
To the lowest depths of the Pit.

Isaiah 14:12–15

Forced to receive him, the earth reacted with repulsion:

Those who see you will gaze at you,
And consider you, saying:
"Is this the man who made the earth tremble,
Who shook kingdoms,
Who made the world as a wilderness
And destroyed its cities,
Who did not open the house of his prisoners?"

Isaiah 14:16–17

In the divine plan of God, Lucifer had been created to oversee a third of the lesser heavenly creatures, leading them in perpetual worship. As he did so, he must have started comparing his role to the role of the One he was worshiping, and eventually he rose up in pride, aspiring to rise above his delegated sphere of authority and to become an equal to God ("I will be like the Most High").

With that expression of pride, he fell, just as the proverb describes: "Pride goes before destruction, and a haughty spirit before a fall" (Proverbs 16:18).

Authority Transfers

So much for the inappropriate seizure of God's authority. How is it that God makes legitimate transfers of His authority to the ones He chooses? Before we can talk about exercising authority over demons, we have to understand how legitimate authority works.

Way back in the Garden, God commissioned Adam, and thereby all of humankind, to rule over the rest of what He had created. God said, "Let Us make man in Our image, according to Our likeness; and let them rule over the fish of the sea and over the birds of the sky and over the cattle and over all the earth, and over every creeping thing that creeps on the earth" (Genesis 1:26, NASB). He made the first humans, and then He blessed them, saying, "Be fruitful and multiply, and fill the earth, and subdue it; and rule over the fish of the sea and over the birds of the sky and over every living thing that moves on the earth" (Genesis 1:28, NASB).

The Father, Son and Holy Spirit had the authority to create and the authority to rule. They had the freedom to delegate that authority if they wished to do so, and that is what they did. They did not transfer the *ownership* of the earth to human beings, but they did transfer the authority to rule over it, use it and take care of it. The earth and the fullness thereof remained in God's own possession. As long as human beings remained aligned with Him, they would be able to exercise their delegated Kingdom dominion with wisdom, according to His will. Adam and Eve had been made in His exact likeness, and they would exercise dominion with holy, sinless authority.

But what happened? Alas, disobedience caused a separation between God and the people He had made (see Genesis 2:17; 3:6–11, 22–23). In effect, the man and the woman chose to proclaim the serpent as their new lord, thus ceding their heaven-bestowed authority to Satan and becoming his slaves (see Romans 6:16).

After that time, human beings belonged to the enemy. Although Satan sometimes appeared to have become the owner of the world, he had not. He was more like a magistrate or administrator, and by definition, his term of authority was going to be a limited one. Nevertheless, the devil had become the "prince of the power of the air" (Ephesians 2:2), and he had the legal right to control the visible realm from his position in the unseen realm.

Then Jesus burst upon the scene. The devil tried to thwart His entrance into the public eye. In the wilderness, Satan tempted Jesus with the very God-given authority that he had stolen from Adam, saying, "All this authority I will give You, and their glory; for this has been delivered to me, and I give it to whomever I wish" (Luke 4:6).

Jesus, however, did not fall for the bait. He knew then what He later declared to His disciples, namely, "All authority in heaven and on earth has been given to me" (Matthew 28:18, NIV). By the time He told them that, He had paid the ransom for humankind. He had bought back His Lordship, becoming the sinless sacrificial Lamb to pay the price for sin-filled humans (see Romans 3:23; 5:8; 6:23; Galatians 3:13–14). Once and for all, Jesus the Son had triumphed over Satan, the one who had usurped the authority of heaven. Disarmed, the devil had been defeated by Jesus, the One who is the Lord over all (see Colossians 2:15; Ephesians 1:17–22; 4:8–9). Now every knee, even the devil's unbending knee, would need to bow before Him (see Romans 14:11).

Full Circle

Within a little over a month of His death and resurrection, Jesus had transferred His authority back to anyone who became filled with His Spirit. After the resurrection, the disciples received the same holy, sinless breath (*pneuma*), or spirit of life, that He possessed (see Genesis 2:7; John 20:22) and the same power (*dunamis*) from on high (see Acts 1:8; Luke 24:49).

From that point forward, the Spirit-led Church could move out, and wherever they went, they could carry God's seal of authority, the authority that prevails over all resistance (see Matthew 28:19–20). The power in them was greater than the power that remained in the world (see 1 John 4:4). Humbly submitted to their living Lord, all they had to do was resist and the enemy would flee (see James 4:7). Now they could pick up the keys to the Kingdom—and use them. Now they could set the captives free from demonic custody (see Mark 16:17).

As a personal aside, let me tell you how directly this can apply to deliverance ministry today. Being submitted to the Lord and filled with His Spirit means that I am indwelt by Someone. I am filled with the Light of God. This bothers the enemy—a lot. Because this is a fact, sometimes when I am ministering to people I just "lean in" and let my light shine. I'm operating in confidence in God, not in myself, because it really has very little to do with me. All I have to do is surrender to the Spirit of Jesus, take hold of the resulting authority that exudes from me and apply it to the situation.

I am not very active, but I am certainly not passive, either. Sometimes I just lean in and have a temporary "stare-down" with a demonized person. I release the light of God that is within me. The darkness absolutely hates this—and it flees. It is like going into a dark room and flipping the light switch without a word; there is no question about the light prevailing over the darkness. All the cockroaches run for cover.

Often I say some words, too, but the most effective part is the light of God within me. My job is to allow the light to conquer the darkness. I do it intentionally. I do not need to repeat commands loudly multiple times or prophesy reams of revelation. The situation may require some determination and perseverance, but it will not require a PhD in deliverance techniques.

We Are Not of This World

You see, we are no longer part of this world. We are no longer subject to its order or hierarchy (see John 15:19; 17:15–16). We are not of this kingdom or realm or rule (see Colossians 1:13). We are not of the world's spirit or disposition (see 1 Corinthians 2:12).

We are in the world but we are not of the "world system." The world system is the temporary cosmic realm ruled from the midheavens by Satan. We are no longer citizens of that realm. We have been given a heavenly transfer card.

In fact, we have been promoted. Satan is a prince, but we are kings! Jesus has made us "kings and priests to His God and Father" (Revelation 1:6). As such, we overrule the god of this world. Our world has become the same as God's world. Our kingdom is His Kingdom. Our spirits belong to His Spirit. No longer can Satan claim us. No longer do we have to drag our chains of bondage. They have been removed and disposed of.

Thanks to this heavenly transfer of authority, you and I have been seated with Christ in heavenly places. What do we do there? We do what kings do—we rule over a domain, over a sphere of authority. That is what we will be exploring in the next chapter.

PART III

Our Authority in Christ

7

Realms of Kingdom Authority

When you and I pray, often we are participating in bigger battles than we realize. While human need, sickness and moral corruption may be obvious to us, we cannot see into the invisible spiritual realm where the prince of darkness hatches evil plots and conspiracies. We fail to appreciate how far-reaching our small efforts may be.

In his book *The Early Christians*, translated from the German, Eberhard Arnold, the theologian and founder of the Bruderhof communities, wrote:

> The son of God became man to destroy demons and the works of the devil. Therefore much more is at stake than the healing of individual people. The vital issue is to purify the earth's atmosphere, to free the entire social and political life, and to completely win our present world-age.
>
> The Christian alone has power over the raging enemy and its host, because he reveals the supreme power of Christ, which the demonic powers have to acknowledge. For every believing Christian is capable of unmasking demons and no demon can

resist his command or persist in any lie. The demons must surrender to the servants of God because they fear Christ in God and God in Christ. In fear, anger, and pain, they abandon their hold when the Crucified is proclaimed.[1]

Every time demonic forces abandon their hold, a little more of the darkness is displaced by the Kingdom of God. Prayers and proclamations of truth make it happen. I believe that the singing of every praise song and the righteous preaching of every sermon displaces a little more. The proclamation of the Gospel is a spiritual weapon that weakens this temporary present darkness that surrounds us.

Spiritual warfare is about individual lives, but also it is about so much more.

Extending Kingdom Authority into Every Sphere of Life

You may have heard about the seven cultural "mountains" of societal influence. These are spheres of influence with which, for the sake of the Kingdom, Christians would do well to engage:

1. Government
2. Education
3. Media
4. Arts and entertainment
5. Religion
6. Family
7. Business

Through their delegated Kingdom authority and energy, every Christian can make a difference in at least a few of these spheres of influence. Wherever their paths take them, ambassadors of the Kingdom can turn the lights on, penetrating the darkness. Suddenly, the works of darkness lie exposed, and reformation ensues. Reformation becomes transformation in pockets of society, and the Kingdom takes root.

This is the proof that the darkness is temporary. With divine ingenuity, inspiration, revelation, interpretation and application, ordinary-seeming believers can make something happen. New life can be released on a daily basis. Remember what Jesus said: "Anyone who has faith in me will do what I have been doing. He will do even greater things than these, because I am going to the Father" (John 14:12, NIV).

Besides these mountains of influence, every Christian can make a difference in a number of other spheres of influence as well.

Extending Kingdom Authority over Demons

Because you have been reading this book, you know without me saying it again that we have the authority to cast out demons. Without "seeing a demon behind every bush," we can nevertheless learn to distinguish demonic fingerprints on the circumstances and affairs of our lives, and we can get rid of the evil spirits who are trying to assert their control.

Extending Kingdom Authority over the Elements

When I mention taking authority over the elements, I think of the time when Jesus calmed the violent storm on the lake (see Mark 4:35–39). Did you know that this is something that you should be able to do, too?

I remember years ago when I was pastor of a church in Missouri, which is located in "Tornado Alley." A giant storm was making a beeline for our little community. Funnel clouds had been spotted; the weather could not have been worse. One of the church elders and his wife called me on the phone and I heard them say, "Aaaaaaahhhhh! It's coming!" I had already had a little bit of success in speaking to storms and commanding them to change, and a spirit of faith rose up in me for this one.

I just spoke to that tornado and I commanded it in Jesus' name to move and go around. It did exactly what I told it to do! (I should have said, "Lift!" The neighbors would have appreciated it.) Afterward, you could see the path of destruction. It followed the beeline up to a certain point, did a little semicircle and then went back to the same track. The winds had obeyed the authority of the Lord Jesus in me.

Extending Kingdom Authority over Natural Laws

This is a little more than taking authority over bad weather—it's taking authority over the natural laws of physics, the principles that govern physical functions such as motion, gravity, chemistry and thermodynamics. Not that you have to know anything about the laws of physics to do it. You only have to know what Jesus is doing so that you can participate in the miracle of it.

The best example of His taking authority over natural law was when He walked on water (see Mark 6:47–48). Then later, He walked through closed doors (see John 20:26 and other gospel accounts). Philip was transported a great distance in an instant, finding himself in Azotus, which was near the ocean, immediately after he had been with the Ethiopian eunuch on the desert road between Jerusalem and Gaza (see Acts 8:26–40).

Others in the Bible—and in modern times—have testified about times when Kingdom authority sweeps over seemingly immutable natural laws.

Extending Kingdom Authority over Temptations

When you are being tempted to sin, you can speak to any enticing spirit who may be summoning you to venture into the darkness. You can command a spirit that is behind a temptation to "bug off," in the name of Jesus. So simple and effective.

Extending Kingdom Authority over Sickness and Death

The gospels are filled with stories about Jesus extending Kingdom authority over sickness and death. Here is a perfect example involving sickness:

> As He entered a village, ten leprous men who stood at a distance met Him; and they raised their voices, saying, "Jesus, Master, have mercy on us!"
>
> When He saw them, He said to them, "Go and show yourselves to the priests." And as they were going, they were cleansed.
>
> Now one of them, when he saw that he had been healed, turned back, glorifying God with a loud voice, and he fell on his face at His feet, giving thanks to Him. And he was a Samaritan.
>
> Then Jesus answered and said, "Were there not ten cleansed? But the nine—where are they? Was no one found who returned to give glory to God, except this foreigner?" And He said to him, "Stand up and go; your faith has made you well."
>
> Luke 17:12–19, NASB

A side note: If you had been living at that time and in that place, you would have expected the lepers to not only keep their distance but also to cry out "Unclean! Unclean!" as they saw people approaching (see Leviticus 13:45). Instead, they cried out, "Jesus, Master, have mercy on us!"—and He did. The authority of God, which is driven by mercy, overruled sickness, decay and death. Moreover, it was a Samaritan who got healed and who returned to thank the Lord Jesus. Even the Samaritans who were not lepers did not mix with Jews. Jesus' mercy and Jesus' authority triumphed over both social ostracism and disfiguring illness. The history of the Church right up to the present moment is filled with similar accounts.

The classic biblical example of the effectiveness of Jesus' authority over death is, of course, the familiar story of Lazarus' resurrection from the dead (see John 11:38–44). Some Bible teachers have theorized that because Jesus carried so much authority, He had to speak Lazarus' name specifically: "Lazarus, come forth!" If He had not, they speculate that many of the other dead people would have come walking out of their tombs!

Extending Kingdom Authority over Finances and Needs

This current time of prolonged financial crisis might be a good occasion to practice extending Kingdom authority over your finances. Jesus did it when He paid an overdue tax bill. He told Peter to go fishing for the money (see Matthew 17:24–27) and the first fish he would catch would have a four-drachma coin in its mouth. With that coin, he could go pay the taxes for both of them.

In a similar way, when we find ourselves laboring under financial difficulties, we can take the opportunity to assert Jesus' authority over our financial deficit. We can call forth blessings and we can call on the Lord to identify and help us capture the malicious thief who has been stealing our provision.

When you are under a financial curse, you feel as if you have a purse with a hole in it. You can almost see the locusts descending on you: "You will sow much seed in the field but you will harvest little, because locusts will devour it" (Deuteronomy 28:38, NIV). But you can call forth discernment and wisdom so that you can sew up the holes in your purse. You can lay claim to additional sources of supply, because the Kingdom of God is not limited to your paycheck. In the authority of the Son of God, you can proclaim that property will sell, that dividends will increase, that wise stewardship will be exercised over your investments.

As the proverb says, when the thief has been identified and captured, he has to repay sevenfold what he took from you (see Proverbs 6:31). Refuse to shoulder the curse of poverty over yourself, your household and even over your generational lineage, in the name of Jesus. Declare that your crisis will change into an opportunity for blessing.

Sometimes you do not need money as much as you need supplies such as food. That is what the crowd of people needed when Jesus multiplied the loaves and fish to feed them (see Matthew 15:32–38; 14:13–21; Mark 6:35–44; 8:1–9; Luke 9:13–17; John 6:1–13). From time to time, you hear contemporary testimonies that rival that one, when not only is food multiplied, but also anything that is under the stewardship of a faith-filled believer. More than once, Heidi and Rolland Baker, missionaries to Mozambique, have seen gifts of toys multiply for the needy and orphaned children in their care.[2]

Speaking of needs, have you ever prayed over your empty gas tank? I have. Amazed, I watched the needle go up from "E" and then I drove away. Now I do not make it a habit to live that way. Normally, I earn money first and then I go to the gas station and buy the gas to fill up my tank. But there are times when I have a need. Next time you are about to run out of gas, try speaking to your gas tank. Command it to fill up. It will never happen unless you do!

Extending Kingdom Authority over Animals

Kingdom authority extends over every form of life that God created: "Then God said, 'Let Us make man in Our image, according to Our likeness; let them have dominion over the fish of the sea, over the birds of the air, and over the cattle, over all the earth and over every creeping thing that creeps on the earth'" (Genesis 1:26). Jesus took Kingdom dominion when He told the discouraged disciples to cast their nets into the water from the right side of the boat instead of the left (see John 21:1–6). Whereas they had not caught as much as a minnow all night long (and remember, these guys were professional fishermen, and they may well have cast their nets from both sides of the boat at different times), now they pulled in a miraculous haul of a hundred and fifty-three fish. It seems that Jesus' authority had caused most of the fish in the Sea of Tiberius to swim into the net right then and there, as if it were a fish-magnet.

(If you cannot get your children to obey you, try your animals. It might just work!)

Extending Kingdom Authority over Fear

Back on the water another time, Jesus' authority was the only thing that worked against the fear of the terrified disciples. That was the time He had been asleep in the stern of the boat in spite of the deluge of rain and the boiling waves (see Mark 4:35–39). At the frantic request of His men, He shook the sleep out of His eyes and spoke the authoritative word, "Quiet! Be still!" The storm ceased. Then He addressed their fear:

> He said to them, Why are you so timid and fearful? How is it that you have no faith (no firmly relying trust)?
>
> And they were filled with great awe and feared exceedingly and said one to another, Who then is this, that even wind and sea obey him?
>
> Mark 4:40–41, AMP

As far as Jesus was concerned, their initial fear was completely unwarranted, because, after all, He was with them. An astonishing thing had just occurred. So they traded fears. They traded their fear of drowning for a healthy fear of the One who could save them from any threat.

Extending Kingdom Authority over Emotions

Fear is a blatant emotion, a good one to be able to overcome (or to convert to healthy fear) through Jesus' authoritative name. But there are many other emotions. Do you suppose Jesus' authority can rein them in, too, when they are out of control? Of course.

Looking at Scripture once again, I see one special account that illustrates how Jesus' own emotions became subject to the loving and merciful jurisdiction of His Father and Spirit. Profound grief had caused Him to withdraw to a solitary place. He just wanted to be alone:

> On Herod's birthday the daughter of Herodias danced for them and pleased Herod so much that he promised with an oath to give her whatever she asked. Prompted by her mother, she said, "Give me here on a platter the head of John the Baptist." The king was distressed, but because of his oaths and his dinner guests, he ordered that her request be granted and had John beheaded in the prison. His head was brought in on a platter and given to the girl, who carried it to her mother. John's disciples came and took his body and buried it. Then they went and told Jesus.
>
> When Jesus heard what had happened, he withdrew by boat privately to a solitary place. Hearing of this, the crowds followed him on foot from the towns. When Jesus landed and saw a large crowd, he had compassion on them and healed their sick.
>
> Matthew 14:6–14, NIV

Jesus' friend and cousin, John, had just been brutally beheaded by the king. Clearly Jesus needed time away from people's demands so that He could recover from His loss. Even according to Jewish tradition, this would have been a time of mourning. Why could the people not respect it?

He tried to get away by boat to the far side of the water, but the people, clamoring for attention, caught wind of His destination and beat Him there, toiling around the lake on foot. Did Jesus throw up His hands in futility or cover His face in despair? Did He tell His friends to push off again and take Him out into the middle of the lake away from everybody? No, He mastered His own crushing grief. He subjugated it to God's higher Kingdom purposes. Although He had not been allowed to release John from prison or to preserve him from a gruesome death, He was fully able to cut short His grieving for the sake of the people, compassionately gathering them to heal them.

Extending Kingdom Authority over Mind and Body

We are seated with Christ Jesus in the heavenly places, far above all rule and authority and dominion and everything that has whatever title you want to give it (see Ephesians 1:20–22). And God "put all things in subjection under His feet, and gave Him as head over all things to the church" (Ephesians 1:22, NASB).

This means that Kingdom authority extends over every mind and everybody that exists now, that ever did exist, and that will exist in the future, human or otherwise. Kingdom authority extends over *all things*, no exceptions. Nothing and nobody is more powerful than God, and the only reason we do not disintegrate when such a powerful force comes to dwell inside us is that He is also the One who makes all things hold together (see Colossians 1:17).

It is all about Him. Or, as He would say, it is all about the Father:

> Do you not believe that I am in the Father, and that the Father is in Me? What I am telling you I do not say on My own authority and of My own accord; but the Father Who lives continually in Me does the (His) works (His own miracles, deeds of power).
>
> John 14:10, AMP

Never Quit

Never forget that you carry within yourself the power and authority of the Savior, who is eternally alive. For that reason, never give up. Never quit.

Those were my wife's final words to me before she went home to be with Jesus. Because Christ, the hope of glory, is in me (see Colossians 1:27), I can keep preaching, teaching and reaching out to people with His light until the day I go home, too. I want to "labor, striving according to His working which works in me mightily" (Colossians 1:29).

In September of 2008, I was scheduled to go to minister with my dear friends Mahesh and Bonnie Chavda at a conference in Fort Mills, South Carolina. My wife was profoundly ill, as she had been for a long time. Before I left, I sat on Michal Ann's bed and told her where I was going. She laid her hand on me and blessed me to go. She told me that she would miss me. I did not know that those would be the last physical words that I would hear from her. Later, our oldest daughter, Grace Ann, went in to see her and she was privileged to hear her mother's last physical words, which were to the effect that she loved her.

On the Saturday afternoon of the conference, I visited the prophet Bob Jones and his wife, Bonnie, so that he could minister to me. One of the things he said was that my wife, Michal Ann, had one last word to give me. I tucked that away and went off to the evening meeting.

As I was sitting in the front row, a woman ran up to me, handed me a blue envelope with a card inside, and I thought she said something about this being a "word from your wife." I glanced at the outside of the card and then I looked around to find the woman who had given it to me, but she had disappeared. I looked for her again the next morning when I was preaching, but I could not find her. I left the card inside my Bible and I forgot about it.

107

When I got home on Sunday night, I discovered that Michal Ann had slipped into a coma. I spent the entire night next to her in the bedroom, which I had not been doing up to that point because she had had health-care services around the clock. In the wee hours of the morning, I surrendered her to the Lord, weeping, and I spoke to her about the word that Bob Jones had given me, praying that she would be able to deliver it to me, although I had no idea how she could transmit one final word to me now. She breathed her last at 7:32 in the morning on September 15, 2008. I completely forgot about Bob's word, I forgot about what I had prayed in the night and I definitely forgot about the blue card.

After two funeral services in two states, I went to Seoul, South Korea, for another scheduled event. I was getting ready to speak, but I really didn't know if I still wanted to keep doing this stuff or not. Everything was so hard. The church was packed. As I got up to speak, somehow I felt the presence of someone that I knew. Without seeing anything or hearing anything, I simply felt the presence of my wife, almost as if God had given her a weekend pass so that she could cheer me on from the balcony as a member of the great cloud of witnesses. It was good for me. I opened my mouth to speak and, to put it in King James English, I waxed eloquent that night. It was some of the best preaching I have ever done.

The next day was the Jewish Day of Atonement, and I always spend that day with the Lord no matter where I am, even if I am in another city or another country. The conference organizers released me so that I could spend the day alone with God. During the night, I ended up having a dream, and in the dream, I was reliving the Saturday night meeting at Mahesh and Bonnie Chavda's conference. There I was, sitting in the front row. In slow motion, someone came up to me, handed me a card and said, in slowed-down speed, "This is a word to you from your wife." Handing me the blue card, the person disappeared. I heard the voice of the Lord saying, "I sent my angel to you to deliver to you your wife's last word."

I woke up (it was 5:00 A.M.), ran to my Bible, found my blue card and opened it. It was now three weeks since my wife had gone home to be with Yeshua. I remembered the outside of the card: "Never, never, never give up." But now I opened the card so that I could read the inside, and it was a personal word for me and our four kids: "I will never, never, never, never stop cheering for you." That was exactly what had happened the night before when I had felt as if I had a personal cheerleader in the balcony.

Interestingly, the card was just a Hallmark card and it had been manufactured in either Kansas City or Toronto, Canada, two of the places that my wife and I had some of our greatest ministry together. God had sent it to me and He made sure I kept it and read it.

The message on the front of that card is a word to every one of us. It is a word of spiritual warfare, a word about exercising Kingdom authority. "Never, never, never give up." That card has become a tool of spiritual warfare for me, and I believe the message on it can be a tool for you as well.

Never-Quit Scriptures

As you move in the power and authority of Jesus, you are actively guarding your life and the lives of your family and friends. You are bringing light into the darkness, and the darkness is not going to overcome it. Here are some passages of Scripture that will fortify you:

> This command I entrust to you, Timothy, my son, in accordance with the prophecies previously made concerning you, that by them you fight the good fight, . . . I have fought a good fight, I have finished my course, I have kept the faith.
>
> 1 Timothy 1:18, NASB; 2 Timothy 4:7, KJV

Be self-controlled and alert. Your enemy the devil prowls around like a roaring lion looking for someone to devour. Resist him, standing firm in the faith, because you know that your brothers throughout the world are undergoing the same kind of sufferings.

1 Peter 5:8–9, NIV

Therefore, do not throw away your confidence, which has a great reward. For you have need of endurance, so that when you have done the will of God, you may receive what was promised.

Hebrews 10:35–36, NASB

Therefore put on the full armor of God, so that when the day of evil comes, you may be able to stand your ground, and after you have done everything, to stand. Stand firm then, with the belt of truth buckled around your waist, with the breastplate of righteousness in place.

Ephesians 6:13–14, NIV

But we are not of those who shrink back and are destroyed, but of those who believe and are saved.

Hebrews 10:39, NIV

Thanks be to God, who gives us the victory through our Lord Jesus Christ. Therefore, my beloved brethren, be steadfast, immovable, always abounding in the work of the Lord, knowing that your labor is not in vain in the Lord.

1 Corinthians 15:57–58

And I say also unto thee, That thou art Peter, and upon this rock I will build my church; and the gates of hell shall not prevail against it. And I will give unto thee the keys of the kingdom of heaven: and whatsoever thou shalt bind on earth shall be bound in heaven: and whatsoever thou shalt loose on earth shall be loosed in heaven.

Matthew 16:18–19, KJV

Yet in all these things we are more than conquerors through Him who loved us.

Romans 8:37

For whatever is born of God overcomes the world. And this is the victory that has overcome the world—our faith.

1 John 5:4

Now thanks be to God who always leads us in triumph in Christ, and through us diffuses the fragrance of His knowledge in every place.

2 Corinthians 2:14

Ye are of God, little children, and have overcome them: because greater is he that is in you, than he that is in the world.

1 John 4:4, KJV

They overcame him
    by the blood of the Lamb
    and by the word of their testimony;
they did not love their lives so much
    as to shrink from death.

Revelation 12:11, NIV

"No weapon formed against you shall prosper,
    And every tongue which rises against you in judgment
    You shall condemn.
    This is the heritage of the servants of the LORD,
    And their righteousness is from Me,"
Says the LORD.

Isaiah 54:17

As we look to Scripture and to the lessons learned by those who have gone before us, we must keep in mind that what worked then will work again. Remember the principle of following the Holy Spirit and depending upon His grace rather than religious methodology and routine only.

Let us exercise the dominion of Jesus Christ in the earth today, letting His will be done, right here and right now, as it is in heaven. Let His Kingdom light extend into and reign over every area of life, permeating this temporary present darkness. That is the truth—the present spiritual darkness is temporary—but only because of you and me and all of the others who carry the Light of Christ inside.

8

Preparations for Deliverance

First comes repentance, then comes deliverance. Before we can start discussing how to achieve deliverance from evil spirits, we must explore what it means to truly repent.

The word *repentance* in the New Testament comes from the Greek word *metanoia*, which means "a change of mind." It includes not only an inward change of attitude and focus but also a change of outward lifestyle and behavior. Repentance is more than feeling sorry for your sins. It means making a break with evil deeds and starting to do good deeds.

The concept of repentance was firmly established in Hebrew culture by the time of Jesus, built on centuries of prophetic words and obedience to God. For example, Isaiah had charged his listeners with these words:

> Wash yourselves, make yourselves clean;
> Put away the evil of your doings from before My eyes.
> Cease to do evil,
> Learn to do good;
> Seek justice,

Rebuke the oppressor;
Defend the fatherless,
Plead for the widow.

Isaiah 1:16–17

That is repentance in action.

Daniel had given advice to Nebuchadnezzar, which could well be applied to the culture of today:

Therefore, O king, may my advice be pleasing to you: break away now from your sins by doing righteousness and from your iniquities by showing mercy to the poor, in case there may be a prolonging of your prosperity.

Daniel 4:27, NASB

Repentance was not a popular message then and it is not a popular message now. When John the Baptist cried out "Repent!" to the people who followed him into the Judean desert, he had to send many of them back because he saw in them no indications that they had made a true change of heart. He was looking for signs that people had repented of their "me-first" attitude. When John told them, "Produce fruit in keeping with repentance" (Luke 3:8, NIV), and the people asked him what he was expecting of them, he answered, "The man with two tunics should share with him who has none, and the one who has food should do the same" (Luke 3:11, NIV). Such generosity would be a fruit in keeping with repentance, evidence that someone's heart had truly changed.

In spite of the number of people who did not bear the fruit of repentance, many people did hear John's message and turn from their sins. In a very real way, John prepared the way for Jesus. How can we tell? As soon as Jesus emerged from the wilderness and began His public ministry, demons began to manifest themselves and depart (see Mark 1:15, 27, 32–34, 39). This was extraordinary.

So as Jesus ministered to people, the message stayed the same: Repent. Change. His disciples preached that message, too. When the thousands responded on the Day of Pentecost by asking "What shall we do?" Peter and the other apostles responded, "Repent, and let every one of you be baptized in the name of Jesus Christ for the remission of sins; and you shall receive the gift of the Holy Spirit" (Acts 2:38). When Paul described to King Agrippa his ministry from the time the Lord had first called him, his summary echoed both John the Baptist and Jesus:

> O King Agrippa, I was not disobedient unto the heavenly vision, but made known openly first of all to those at Damascus, then at Jerusalem and throughout the whole land of Judea, and also among the Gentiles, that they should repent and turn to God, and do works and live lives consistent with and worthy of their repentance.
>
> Acts 26:19–20, AMP

When people live reformed lives consistent with repentance, their common bond with darkness gets broken. After that, deliverance gets easier. Thanks to repentance, the enemy loses his grip. The person who has repented is in a better position to receive further deliverance.

In its broadest sense, deliverance means having a free heart. If you have been delivered, you have been set free from fear, shame, blame and much more. Eventually, after the exit of evil spirits and subsequent internal cleaning-up from their activities, you can say that you are "free indeed" (see John 8:36).

Steps to Crowd Out Evil Spirits

In essence, a reformed lifestyle leaves very little room for evil spirits. People who are filled with God's light do not provide a welcoming environment for spirits of darkness.

The best way to show evil spirits the door is to continue to repent and change for the better. Specifically, you need to renounce all idolatry; God will show you what that entails in your own life. You also need to give up anything having to do with the occult and false religions. You need to break away from sexual immorality and all immoral relationships. Abandoning pretense, you need to humble yourself under God's hand and be honest with Him, with yourself and with other people, sometimes confessing specific sins. You need to forgive—often and deeply. As God shows you where you have maintained a "me-first" attitude, you must surrender to the control and Lordship of Jesus Christ, turning from all rebellion and from speaking evil against God or His delegated authorities in your life. I want to expand on each of these steps in some detail.

Renounce Idolatry, the Occult and False Religions

The Lord calls us into full love and intimacy with Himself, and His words in the Ten Commandments still apply today:

> You shall have no other gods before me.
>
> You shall not make for yourself an idol in the form of anything in heaven above or on the earth beneath or in the waters below. You shall not bow down to them or worship them; for I, the LORD your God, am a jealous God, punishing the children for the sin of the fathers to the third and fourth generation of those who hate me, but showing love to a thousand [generations] of those who love me and keep my commandments.
>
> Exodus 20:3–6, NIV

Idolatry means putting any person, thing or spirit before God, and that includes putting yourself and your ideas ahead of Him. This is not just an outmoded Old Testament concept. Paul termed covetousness idolatry: "For this you know with certainty, that no immoral or impure person or covetous man, who is an idolater, has an inheritance in the kingdom of Christ and God" (Ephesians 5:5, NASB).

Idolatry is a serious form of sin, because it is really a worship of self instead of God. Paul's prescription for idolatry was severe: "Put to death, therefore, whatever belongs to your earthly nature: sexual immorality, impurity, lust, evil desires and greed, which is idolatry" (Colossians 3:5, NIV). To break away from idolatry, we are expected to get rid of anything that is associated with it.

The Old Testament records wholesale purges of the things that were associated with idolatry, which included occult paraphernalia, all abominable cult practices and people who were spiritists (see 1 Kings 15:12; 2 Kings 23:24). Failure to comply with God's Law meant that the curse of Exodus 20:5 kicked in. Joshua experienced it firsthand when Israel was defeated at Ai because they had maintained common ground with the enemy (see Joshua 7).

The categories of idolatry, the occult and false religions overlap because all of them involve a substitution of another god for the one true God. Yet occult practices and the doctrines of false religions are easier to discern than the hidden aspects of idolatry. "Occult" is a general word that refers to making contact with the supernatural world by any means other than by the Spirit of Jesus Christ, often using secret knowledge and carrying paranormal associations. History is filled with the occult and false religions. A sampling from our own day would include New Age crystals and channeling, Ouija boards, astrology and horoscopes, fortune-telling, séances, mediums, spiritists, ESP (extrasensory perception), astral projection, Theosophy, the teachings of Elizabeth Clare Prophet and the Ascended Masters, Taoism and the realm of Satanism and satanic cults, neopagan cults, Wicca, voodoo, witchcraft and secret societies, such as Freemasonry. In Deuteronomy 18:9–14, God prohibits all such practices.

Bible teacher Derek Prince subdivided the occult into three categories:

1. *Sorcery.* Entering the supernatural realm by means of music, drugs, powders, incantations, incense, chanting and so forth.
2. *Divination.* Divining or discovering information about people, events, things or the future by using astrology, tarot cards, spirit guides, palm-reading, ESP, tea leaves and so forth.
3. *Witchcraft.* One person controlling another person by means of a spirit other than the Holy Spirit, which could include curses, hexes and control spirits (i.e., controlling through fear, guilt, terror or the like).

If you have attempted to control another person, you should repent of the sin of witchcraft. In addition—and this is easily missed—you should release in Jesus' name all of the individuals you have tried to control. This is a way of "moving in the opposite spirit." Instead of retaining a degree of control for your own soulish gain, you release and bless others. Failure to adequately repent and reform results in a continuation of deep occult bondage, which, as we have already noted, can be passed down to succeeding generations:

And when the people [instead of putting their trust in God] shall say to you, Consult for direction mediums and wizards who chirp and mutter, should not a people seek and consult their God? Should they consult the dead on behalf of the living? [Direct such people] to the teaching and to the testimony! If their teachings are not in accord with this word, it is surely because there is no dawn and no morning for them.
And they [who consult mediums and wizards] shall pass through [the land] sorely distressed and hungry; and when they

118

are hungry, they will fret, and will curse by their king and their God; and whether they look upward or look to the earth, they will behold only distress and darkness, the gloom of anguish, and into thick darkness and widespread, obscure night they shall be driven away.

Isaiah 8:19–22, AMP

As you can see, idolatry, the occult and false religion are broader than having a random Buddha statue on your shelf. Right straight through the New Testament, the ancient cause-and-effect curse still applied, although with Jesus' advent, the multigenerational curse could finally be broken. God commanded the early Christians make a clean break with anything associated with idolatry or occult beliefs (see Revelation 2:14, 20). They burned all scrolls and items associated with sorcery (see Acts 19:19). To counteract covetousness, they sold their possessions to meet the needs of the community and to offer help to the poor (see Luke 3:10–11; Acts 4:32–35; 2 Corinthians 8:3–15). No longer were they "me-centered." They had broken off the long-standing curse.

At any point, righteousness can start to take root in a family line, replacing sin. Righteousness may not have much of a history in your own family tree, but you can be the one who changes that pattern. You can be the one who breaks off the curse that has followed you through your ancestors, and it will be broken for good. If God is showing you something in your own life that amounts to idolatry, renounce it. Repent. Turn away. Ask for a fresh infilling of His Spirit to replace the darkness. Get a clear idea of what your idolatry consisted of, and do not even stand in the draft of it anymore. Steer clear of anything associated with the unrighteousness that used to be so familiar to you. If you used to be addicted to pornography, get rid of your computer if you have to. Better to have no computer than to be held in the bondage of sin (see Matthew 5:30).

When true repentance occurs, the fruit of sin dries up. The devil gets starved out. He has nothing to feed on anymore. To become truly free, it is essential to renounce these areas specifically as sin. It is also necessary to destroy amulets, books and objects associated with the occult, lest the spirits have a portal of entry into your home or your life.

Sexual Immorality and All Immoral Relationships

To close more portals of entry into your life, you need to repent of and shun all premarital or adulterous sexual relationships, incest, homosexuality, lesbianism, bestiality, habitual masturbation, prostitution and the use of pornography. Paul had to write to the Corinthian Christians about sexual sin. "Do you not know that your bodies are members of Christ? Shall I then take away the members of Christ and make them members of a prostitute? May it never be!" (1 Corinthians 6:15, NASB) (see also Leviticus 18:6, 20, 22–23; Matthew 5:27–28; 1 Corinthians 6:9–11; 2 Peter 2:14).

Some people say, "All sin is the same," and it is true in the sense that all sin cuts us off from fellowship with God. But different types of sin carry differing consequences, in your own life and in the lives of others. Sexual sin is problematic because, unlike other types of sin, which are committed outside one's body, sexual sin is committed against one's own body. Sexual sin is a form of self-hatred. Sexual sin holds the door open wide to demonic invasion.

Another very interesting aspect of the far-reaching tentacles of sexual sin can be observed when a spiritual leader is walking in immorality, in which case his or her sin is introducing sin into not only specific physical bodies, but also into the body of the Church. A spiritual leader who is walking in immorality is holding open the door of a congregation or even an entire denomination to an incursion of evil. Divorce and marital problems will run rampant in such a body of believers, and they will not understand why. The consequences of the leader's sin have greater impact than the consequences of the same type of sin in a member of the congregation. This is not simply because the leader models sin, but more because the leader has sinned against his own body, holding open a door to immoral behavior that should have been bolted shut.

Humble Yourself

A very basic step toward crowding out the presence of evil in your life is to humble yourself. The Bible is clear about this one:

> Everyone who exalts himself will be humbled, but he who humbles himself will be exalted.
>
> Luke 18:14, NASB

> Humble yourselves [feeling very insignificant] in the presence of the Lord, and He will exalt you [He will lift you up and make your lives significant].
>
> James 4:10, AMP

> Be clothed with humility, for
>
> > God resists the proud,
> > But gives grace to the humble.
> >
> > 1 Peter 5:5

> Humble yourselves, therefore, under God's mighty hand, that he may lift you up in due time. Cast all your anxiety on him because he cares for you. Be self-controlled and alert. Your enemy the devil prowls around like a roaring lion looking for someone to devour.
>
> 1 Peter 5:6–8, NIV

Notice that nowhere does the Bible indicate that God will humble you. Instead, the responsibility lies with you yourself. Humility is a choice. When you humble yourself, you choose to lower yourself in submission to God. You acknowledge His superiority; you apply to Him for help. Often where deliverance is concerned, you will have a choice of keeping your dignity and your demons or losing your dignity (perhaps)—and also your demons. Humility figures into the picture when you hear a statement such as, "Deliverance is for the desperate."

Humility is not the same as humiliation, which carries an element of shame and condemnation and which is a tactic of the devil. To be humble simply means that you are not proud, haughty, arrogant or assertive. You are unpretentious and deferential, especially to God, recognizing that you are very small in comparison to Him.

Be Honest

In preparation for deliverance, it always helps to be honest. Straightforward honesty is the opposite of the confusing and seductive lies and insinuations of the enemy.

Honesty puts you in the light. It is the opposite of concealing your transgressions (see Proverbs 28:13). Honesty implies openness. When you are honest, you are not worried about making yourself vulnerable. You are not confessing your sin but failing to cease and desist (therefore hiding it away for another day). Your honesty is certainly not going to embarrass God, who knows everything already.

As a sign of honesty, the Bible suggests that you find a trustworthy person to whom you confess your sins, so that the person can pray for you and you will be delivered from your sin (see James 5:16). If you commit yourself to walk in the light with God and with others, you will be rewarded with freedom (see 1 John 1:7; Ephesians 4:25; 5:8–13; 6:14).

Confess Specific Sins to Whomever Assists in Deliverance

I cited Proverbs 28:13 just above. It reads, "He who conceals his transgressions will not prosper, but he who confesses and forsakes them will find compassion" (NASB).

When you confess directly to the person or persons who will be praying for your deliverance (and whom, presumably, you can trust), you are paving the way to your own freedom. Scripture tells us, "Therefore confess your sins to each other and pray for each other so that you may be healed. The prayer of a righteous man is powerful and effective" (James 5:16, NIV).

Be thorough but brief, not dwelling on explicit details but identifying them honestly and with brokenness and true repentance (see Acts 19:18; 1 John 1:7–9).

Forgive

I cannot overstress the importance of this one. Forgiveness is one of the highest weapons of spiritual warfare. Unforgiveness blocks your prayers from being answered. Failure to forgive allows demons to retain their legal right to torment (see Matthew 18:34–35; Mark 11:25–26; 2 Corinthians 2:10–11).

When you forgive, you cut off many of the enemy's supply lines, making possible deliverance from oppression he has perpetrated. For complete freedom, you must forgive anyone who has wronged or hurt you, and keep forgiving others as new circumstances warrant (see Matthew 18:21–22; Luke 23:34).

In the Lord's Prayer, the model prayer, we first confess our trespasses as we forgive those who trespass against us. The very next line is "deliver us from evil" (see Matthew 6:12–15). The sequence is as significant as the connection between the two steps.

Ask for Forgiveness and Make Restitution

If you have wronged others, promise to ask for forgiveness and also to make restitution if necessary (and if possible). To promote a climate of peace, seek reconciliation between estranged parties (see Matthew 5:23–25; Acts 24:16; Romans 12:18).

Our human tendency is to withhold true forgiveness and to hold on to blame toward other people for doing something wrong. It is easy to go to other people, tell them everything they did wrong (which they may not have realized until that moment) and then to tack on an insincere word of forgiveness. That is not asking for forgiveness and it is not redemptive; it is casting stones of blame and shame instead. When you do that, you subject yourself to further bondage and you become a conduit of criticism toward someone instead of a conveyor of wholeness.

We need to move from vertical forgiveness (between ourselves and God) toward increased horizontal forgiveness (mutual forgiveness between people). Without waiting for the other party to come to you, take the initiative and go to him or her instead. Express yourself in such a way as to make it clear that you are not demanding the other person to receive every word you say.

When circumstances require and permit it, we also need to make appropriate restitution. Remember what Zacchaeus did (see Luke 19:8–10). He not only received the Lord's forgiveness and acceptance, he also took the initiative to repay up to quadruple what he had defrauded people of. What a good example of horizontal reconciliation and restitution and a truly changed heart. I am sure that Zacchaeus's actions discouraged any demonic powers from remaining attached to him.

Turn from Rebellion and Speaking Evil toward God and All Delegated Authority

Submit to authority wherever you meet it, whether toward God, in the Church or in the secular world (see 1 Samuel 15:23; Romans 13:1–2; 1 Peter 2:13). Let no evil talk come out of your mouth; do not grumble or chafe under the constraints that leaders place upon you (see James 5:9; Ephesians 4:29).

Humble submission to authority is as much a way of building a hedge of protection around your life as it is a preparation for deliverance.

Surrender to the Lordship of Jesus in Every Area of Life

On your final victory lap, release all of the things over which you have control and relinquish your right to control other people or circumstances. Surrender your rights, giving them to the Lord of your life.

Often by the time a person gets through all of these steps toward crowding out the devil, that person will be free already. When demonic entities no longer have squatter's rights, they may pack up and leave or be ready to leave the next time they are denied power, influence or privileges. May this be your personal experience of deliverance!

Discerning the Enemy

After you have loosened the grip of the enemy in your life (or in the life of another person who is seeking deliverance from evil spirits), how do you prepare to finalize the deliverance? How do you figure out which impulses come from an evil spirit and which come from the human spirit or the Holy Spirit? You can tell what evil spirits are up to by a number of means.

Word of Knowledge

Often when I am praying for someone for deliverance, the Holy Spirit drops into my mind or heart the name or identifying characteristic of the evil spirit at hand. This may come to me in the form of a thought, an image or the feeling of their torment.

I believe that much can be learned by making genealogical queries to determine patterns of iniquity in the person's family. Is there a history of divorce? Criminal activity? Addictions? Satanic ritual abuse? Yet often at the time of deliverance, it comes down to a word of knowledge.

Discerning of Spirits

By the spiritual gift of discerning of spirits, you can recognize what kind of spirit is at work—Holy Spirit, human spirit or evil spirit. The recognition of an evil spirit can entail seeing the actual demon (with your "spirit eyes") or its method of demonic torment. Discernment can also come in the form of smells, tastes or sensations in certain parts of the body.

"Name Yourself"

When an unclean spirit has been detected, but it is resisting eviction, you may find it helpful to command the spirit to name itself. Then you can move from general prayer to targeted warfare against that particular spirit. Some people do this as a rule, although I do not. Of course the precedent in Scripture is when Jesus commanded the spirit in the Gerasene demoniac to name itself and it replied, "Legion" (see Mark 5:9). That was a situation in which the lead demon's name was all that was required to cast out all of the lesser demons under his command.

I once had a remarkable experience that illustrates this method. I was ministering with Mahesh Chavda in what was then Yugoslavia, right after the 1984 Winter Olympics were held in Sarajevo. Mahesh was handling the evening healing meetings, and he had asked me to follow him around and provide extra prayer for people. I had an interpreter with me in case I wanted to speak directly to a person.

A college student was down on the floor and he was stiff and motionless. His extremities were turning so cold that they were blue. He was curled up in a ball, sort of paralyzed. I could tell that there were some sexual issues and other things, but I simply could not get any discernment on the situation. I was praying in tongues, waiting for a word of knowledge, anything that would help.

Finally, I decided to command the strong man (the lead spirit) to identify itself. I knew that if I could take the strong man, I could take his plunder (see Matthew 12:29; Mark 3:27; Luke 11:22). Naturally, I was speaking English, and I did not even know what language the student spoke. Much to my astonishment, the young man spoke—in English!—saying, "Take the book out."

"Take the book out"? What was that supposed to mean? I looked in his hip pocket, and there was a copy of *Mein Kampf* by Adolf Hitler. I removed the book from his pocket and all of the demons left him in a moment. It was a miracle. Then he was born again and filled with the Holy Spirit.

A little later he was standing up, no longer blue, stiff or paralyzed. In fact, he was so exhilarated that he appeared to be inebriated. I asked my interpreter what was happening. He told me what the young man was saying: "Your Jesus gets me higher than any drug I've ever been on before." He turned out to be a philosophy major from Hungary who was studying at the University of Sarajevo, and he did not speak a word of English. That was the first time that English had ever come out of his mouth.

Observe Behaviors

People with experience in praying for deliverance can often detect the presence and activity of demons by ordinary observation. Behaviors that might at other times be perfectly normal give away the demonic presence. Indicative behaviors can include the following:

- Restlessness, rapid eye movement
- Extreme talkativeness, specifically verbal abuse
- Escape/flight patterns
- Obsessive-compulsive habits and addictions (drugs, alcohol, pornography/masturbation, gambling, caffeine, overeating, television, etc.)
- Continued failure overcoming sins, even after prayer and fasting and seeking God
- Recurring unclean thoughts or illicit sex acts
- Involvement in the occult, Satanism, false religions or Christian cults

Let me add a word of explanation about a couple of these. By "escape/flight patterns," I mean people who are overly attracted to fantasy and escapism because they just have to run away from reality. These are the people who quit their college classes, switch majors several times, fail to finish their jobs, dump their boyfriends or girlfriends or move from city to city in a search for satisfaction. The pattern of their behavior shows deep-seated roots of rejection and failure to receive the Father's love. By dealing with the roots, you can unseat any demons who may be taking a free ride.

By "continued failure overcoming sins, even after prayer and fasting and seeking God," I mean that these people are attacking the wrong root or using the wrong weapon. You can crucify the sinful flesh—but you cannot crucify a demon. You can cast out a demon—but you cannot cast out the flesh.

Confidentiality and Love

In deliverance, the issue of confidentiality should go without saying, but it is so important that it bears repeating. When you are praying for a person who is oppressed by evil spirits, your main focus should be pleasing Jesus, always watching your heart so that you do not fall into criticism or judgment. The gift of the discerning of spirits is not the gift of gossip!

Love and compassion go a long way. We are dealing with fellow human beings who happen to be afflicted with evil spirits, people who should not be painted with the same brush as the unclean spirits.

Oftentimes people who need deliverance are difficult to love. Frank Hammond's book, *Pigs in the Parlor*, has become a classic manual about deliverance. He addresses this delicate topic:

> The very people most needful of deliverance are often the most difficult to love. They may turn on us and offend us when we offer compassion and love. But we are commanded to love even those who seem least worthy of love (cf. Matthew 5:43–48). In fact, this is exactly the way God delivered us. He loved us even though we were altogether unlovely (cf. Romans 5:8). His love broke down our barriers and his love has the power to break down every spiritual wall. Love is a powerful weapon in the hands of a skilled spiritual warrior.[1]

When you minister deliverance to others, remember that "love covers a multitude of sins" (1 Peter 4:8, NASB). Above all, communicate the forgiveness and acceptance of Jesus. For best results, work with a team of two or three trusted people, all of whom have committed themselves to walk in confidentiality (see Proverbs 25:9–10).

Look to Jesus as your model. Jesus ministered deliverance to many people, but He never condemned any of them. Love and compassion motivated Him, always, as He touched the people of Judea. It still does today, through you and through me.

9

Effective Procedures for Deliverance

In this chapter I am going to address the topic of deliverance as if you are the person who is ministering it to another. Although I will try to cover all of the practical procedures and cautions possible, you should keep in mind that no single chapter (or entire book, for that matter) can address every aspect of such a topic. Many other helpful resources exist, a few of which I refer to throughout this book, and the main message you should take away from this chapter is that learning to minister deliverance is a lifelong endeavor. Where deliverance from evil spirits is concerned, experience is the best teacher. As you follow the Holy Spirit and try not to get in over your head, do not be afraid of situations that will challenge and stretch you.

He will lead you. All you need to do is to follow. While it is very helpful to be familiar with wisdom gleaned by others, the most important "procedure" to learn is how to follow the often-subtle direction of God's Holy Spirit. Jesus is the Deliverer; we are His followers. He reminds us that "apart from Me you can do nothing" (John 15:5, NASB; see also Matthew 12:28).

Practical Points for Ministering Deliverance

Beyond the underlying, all-important point of being led by the Spirit of God, I want to list for you a number of practical points that will help you minister deliverance effectively.

Minister in Private, in a Team

If possible—and it is not always possible—seek to minister deliverance in a private setting. The safest environment includes a small team of trusted people, each of whom will have certain strengths.

One reason for privacy involves the enemy's penchant for drawing attention to himself. He loves gawkers (see Mark 9:25). Often in a public gathering, demons will act up and manifest themselves by making noises, producing strange behaviors or otherwise creating a spectacle. This is never helpful.

Having a small team of people provides extra protection as well as efficiency and an increased ability to hear the Lord's instructions. Having a team—either all of the same gender as the person receiving ministry, or a mixed-gender group—also circumvents the very real problems that can arise when an individual man ministers to an individual woman or vice versa. If you cannot find other team members, never minister one-on-one across gender lines, which transgresses boundaries and is just asking for trouble.

Encourage Fasting

Because the Lord Jesus told us that some evil spirits will not depart without prayer and fasting (see Mark 9:29), fasting is simply a good precautionary policy. When the deliverance session has been planned ahead of time, people have an opportunity to fast. Not only is it smart to fast yourself, it can be even more helpful to ask the candidate to fast beforehand. Fasting prepares hearts and makes people much more open to receiving from God.

Create an Atmosphere of Soaking Worship

This can be as simple as playing a CD of worship music in the background, beginning before the team arrives in the room at the appointed time. A worshipful atmosphere will help set people's expectation on the Lord Himself. Worship generates a creative environment that is conducive to prayer.

During the time of deliverance prayer, maintain an atmosphere of gentle joy, peace, praise and worship. Prior to confrontational prayer, make sure that thanksgiving prevails in the room. We enter His gates with thanksgiving and His courts with praise (see Psalm 100). This aspect of deliverance prayer is often overlooked.

In the light of preparing a beneficial atmosphere for deliverance prayer, look at the following familiar advice from Scripture:

> Rejoice in the Lord always. I will say it again: Rejoice! Let your gentleness be evident to all. The Lord is near. Do not be anxious about anything, but in everything, by prayer and petition, with thanksgiving, present your requests to God. And the peace of God, which transcends all understanding, will guard your hearts and your minds in Christ Jesus.
>
> Philippians 4:4–7, NIV

Dealing with a Stalemate

During the ministry time, you are likely to encounter an impasse. When progress seems to be at a standstill and you sense that there is some kind of blockage, be sure to check for (1) remaining unforgiveness, (2) unconfessed sins, (3) soul ties or (4) demons of dumbness.

Where remaining unforgiveness is concerned, ask God to drop into the person's mind any further names of people whom they need to forgive. The Bible tells us that the heart knows its own bitterness (see Proverbs 14:10), so this kind of information can come right from the person's own memories, but even that sort of thing can be supernaturally induced through prayer. The Holy Spirit will spark what I call divine intelligence, revealing names or situations for which forgiveness is necessary.

A stalemate can sometimes be traced to a hidden sin such as past cult involvement, sexual sins or abortion (which should be confessed as murder). Confessing sins that were previously hidden can release freedom.

Soul ties can be one of the major blocks to receiving freedom. Soul ties include emotional ties to other people that are outside of Jesus Christ, which is to say human ties in which either party controlled the other. Soul ties are somewhat like an umbilical cord. Most often, soul ties are implicated in illicit sexual liaisons. Until a person is able to break a soul tie and release the other person, demons have a legal right to remain.

Demons of dumbness hinder speech. They cause forgetfulness, confusion and sometimes mocking, hysterical laughter. Naturally, this type of spirit inhibits the person receiving deliverance from participating fully. If you identify a demon of dumbness (sometimes known as a "deaf and dumb spirit"), simply cast it out of the place in Jesus' name.

To break a stalemate, especially if it continues after you have tried one of these approaches, you might decide to spend some time praising and worshiping the Lord together. Minister to Jesus, proclaiming His victory by the blood of His cross and His resurrection. Then wait awhile until the Holy Spirit gives further direction.

Times of Holy Spirit Delay

Some slowdowns are not attributable to demonic hindrance; sometimes they have been instituted by the Holy Spirit Himself, as if He has pushed a "pause" button.

The Spirit is not in a hurry. He knows the outcome, and the enemy is already under His feet. It has been said that patience starves out the devil, and this is especially true in situations where inner healing is associated with deliverance.

We have plenty of scriptural precedent for God-instigated slowdowns. For example:

> But I will not drive them out in a single year, because the land would become desolate and the wild animals too numerous for you. Little by little I will drive them out before you, until you have increased enough to take possession of the land.
>
> Exodus 23:29–30, NIV

The person may need to rebuild walls of resistance, learn to use spiritual weapons or learn to exercise self-control. The Holy Spirit wants the person to be able to keep the freedom that has been obtained to date. After the person has consolidated his or her gains, the next steps toward deliverance can be taken. The land is conquered little by little.

Be Yielded to Christ

Above all, go into a deliverance session fully yielded to Jesus Christ, having searched your own heart for pockets of resistance against Him and unforgiveness toward others. Allow the searchlight of the Holy Spirit to probe your motives and to purify them. Are you seeking solely for God's glory? Is your heart moved by love and compassion for the oppressed?

Know Your Limits, Establish Boundaries

Do not let your ministry efforts outstrip your abilities. Just because you may have experience in casting out spirits of fear does not mean that you know what to do when confronted with a situation involving ritual satanic abuse. Even though you can expect to find that you are being "stretched" in your experience, do not get in over your head. Team ministry should provide safeguards.

One of the most delicate types of situations involves praying for deliverance for someone who has been diagnosed with a mental illness. Symptoms and behaviors of mental illness can masquerade as demonic possession and vice versa. Psychiatrists and other medical professionals do not typically have experience with prayer ministry, but you need to partner with them because of their expertise and their ability to manage medications and other medical interventions during the course of a patient's treatment.

The lists below, quoted from the book, *Deliverance and Inner Healing* by John Loren Sandford and his son Mark Sandford, were written with schizophrenics in mind, yet the advice also applies to praying for people who suffer from other mental illnesses:

- Let a mental health professional do the diagnosing.
- Do not deal with a [mental disorder] unless you are a seasoned prayer minister.
- When possible, obtain written approval from the person's psychiatrist stating that he or she is ready for inner healing. Even if he does not share your religious beliefs, the psychiatrist is far more experienced than you at evaluating . . . stability. When needful, report back to him about progress.
- Make sure the person is not presently delusional, or you will only reinforce his defenses. Wait until he has a fairly firm handle on reality (this is one of the purposes of medication).
- Pray for guidance and obtain advice about whether you should minister to this person.

- Make sure the person has a track record of exploring personal issues without experiencing the kind of stress that might trigger a psychotic break.
- In most cases, medication will be needed for a season, until the person can hold on to reality without it. Let the doctor determine when that might be.

If you and the person's doctor decide he is ready to receive inner healing, the following should make prayer ministry stress-relieving, instead of stress-provoking:

- Make clear to the person what you are able to do. If you are not a mental health expert, you cannot target the psychosis itself. Instead, you will deal with the same kinds of issues you would deal with in any average person. . . .
- Whenever possible, encourage the family to become involved in a support group that can help them understand and cope with their loved one's illness.
- Go slowly. Even [someone] with a firm hold on reality might take a little longer to progress.
- Do not pressure him to deal with issues he is not yet secure about facing. . . .
- Be sensitive about the length of sessions. Be aware of that moment when he begins to feel overloaded.
- Keep things simple. Focus on one item at a time.
- Make teaching clear and uncomplicated, checking to make sure the person understands. Even at his best, he may still have some degree of distorted thinking. . . .
- From time to time, check to see if any voices, false ideas or beliefs are distorting his perceptions of what you are sharing.
- Find the emerging person God created. Uncover creativity and enable the person to cast a vision for life.[1]

Whether or not you are praying with someone who has been diagnosed with a mental illness, your goal for the person is the same—freedom in mind, emotions, will and spirit. Being born again does not give anyone a new brain, although everyone can receive the mind of Christ through steady transformation. Prayer for deliverance or inner healing offers further transformation.

The people with whom you pray may need some assistance in identifying ungodly belief patterns—assumptions that are not true. All of us discover such belief patterns from time to time. They come from our childhood, our religious background and our general education. The cure for ungodly beliefs is always the same—unadulterated applications of the Word of God.

Let this imperative statement made originally to the people in the church at Rome apply to you and to those for whom you pray: "And be not conformed to this world: but be ye transformed by the renewing of your mind, that ye may prove what is that good, and acceptable, and perfect, will of God" (Romans 12:2, KJV).

In a chapter about effective procedures for deliverance, the subject of overcoming ungodly belief systems is crucial because a renewed mind is an important defense against the enemy. Even after successful deliverance from evil spirits, too often an unrenewed mind is the same as a broken-down wall around a city—enemies find easy access to regaining control.

In my own life, I learned about this the hard way. Years ago as a young man, I received deliverance from some seemingly entrenched evil spirits. I knew very little about what had happened, and still less about how to protect myself. Later in my life I came to understand that I could shoo the blackbird away from the nest, but unless I tore up the nest, the blackbird would come back to roost again. As I cast them away, I needed to have identified the twigs that made up the nest. I needed to have captured my errant beliefs and thoughts, allowing the power of God to transform them. Paul's advice was sound:

The weapons we fight with are not the weapons of the world. On the contrary, they have divine power to demolish strongholds. We demolish arguments and every pretension that sets itself up against the knowledge of God, and we take captive every thought to make it obedient to Christ.

2 Corinthians 10:4–5, NIV

I didn't do this, and as a result, I did not keep my whole deliverance. I had to start over, discovering this time the roots for the problems and receiving ministry in order to "lay the axe to the root" (see Matthew 3:10). To counter the ungodly beliefs that composed the nest for the enemy, I needed to affirm godly declarations about my life, choosing the opposite spirit, in essence building a "nest" for the Holy Spirit of God to replace the old nesting place. This has proved to be the way out of bondage once and for all.[2]

Procedures for Deliverance

Having established an atmosphere of worship, spend some time discussing the matter at hand. Explain to the person that Jesus Christ can bring freedom, but that personal response is all-important. Nobody can receive freedom from evil spirits or from other persistent problems without a willingness to be free. Make it clear that the person must work honestly with the Holy Spirit and with you. Otherwise, any amount of diagnosis, discernment and prayer will fall short. Some people refer to this time of discussion as the "interview" because through it both parties will become better acquainted with each other.

The initial phase of ministry must cover the basics about salvation and sin. If the person has never received salvation, now is the time to do it. Lead the person in repenting of sin in specific problem areas and also in renouncing sinful activity. Because you are in a position of ministering to another, you are also in a strong position to pronounce forgiveness. You are an ambassador on behalf of God. Speak aloud and declare, "You are forgiven." Add that God is always faithful to forgive confessed sins and to cleanse the heart of the one who repents.

Now you are moving into a more active leading role in the prayer session. After pronouncing the person forgiven, you should further loosen the hold of the enemy by breaking the power of strongholds that resulted from the sinful pattern. You may be able to identify strongholds by a single word or by a description of their effect in the life of the person. Then, in so many words, close off access points to the person's spirit and soul.

Throughout the ministry time, treat the person with dignity. Even in the grip of foul spirits, he or she is someone loved by God. Your highest call is to minister His love to others. Try to remain sensitive to the anointing presence of the Holy Spirit from the beginning of the session to the end. You will never outgrow your need for His anointing. What is more, you will make very little headway without it. Sometimes, in fact, the anointing of the Spirit condenses ten steps into one, making deliverance easy. Throughout the ministry session, resist the tendency to close your eyes prayerfully. Instead, try to maintain eye contact with the person to whom you are ministering, remembering that a person's eyes are the lamp of the body (see Matthew 6:22). With eyes open, manifestations are obvious, including the simple "look" of fear or a demonic presence—or clarity when freedom has been achieved.

Commanding according to God's Commands

When you command evil spirits to come out of a person, you do not need to raise your voice. The spirits are not deaf, and they will not hurry faster because they are alarmed by your volume.

Nevertheless, you can and should use a firm tone of voice, simply because you know your place in Christ and you know your authority. You do not need to be polite, and you will not be making suggestions. You are not allowing the demons to have any options. They must leave, in the mighty name of Jesus.

"Classical" procedure includes the following commands (exclamation points imply firmness, not necessarily loudness):

- "Manifest yourself!"
- "I bind and rebuke you."
- "Silence!"
- "Identify yourself!"
- "(Name), come out in the name of Jesus!"
- "Depart from here and do not return."

More commonly, people minister deliverance by simply saying, "I break the power of (name or function of demon). Come out in the name of Jesus." From time to time, you may need to ask the person to lift up his or her face so that you can look each other in the eye.

Be aware of demons' hiding techniques. Be aware also of the possibility of multiple spirits. You will have more success if you go after the "strongman" (see Matthew 12:29; Mark 3:27), or lead demon. If the lead demon goes down, all the rest will fall like dominoes.

Some spirits leave in such a mild way that their departure is almost unobservable. Others seem so firmly entrenched that you may need to search for the key of release, such as further repentance, a deep inner wound, a curse, a sin in an earlier generation, a vow or the like. Sometimes, the most effective technique is simply to have the person himself or herself call on God for deliverance. When this happens, evil spirits know for a certainty that they cannot stay.

Avoid being snared by the "I've-got-to-get-it-now-because-everybody's-watching" trap. The process may be immediate, or it may not. The candidate usually knows when the demon is gone. Your part is to do another interview and ask questions to find out.

Depending on the nature of the evil, immediately after casting out evil spirits you may decide to employ what is known as "body dedication." Based on Romans 12:1–2, this means presenting the members of one's body to the Lord as His temple. You may want to lead the person in a prayer of surrender to the Lord of hands, eyes, mouth and so forth, especially when spirits of sexual sin have been implicated.

After cleansing from evil spirits, pray for the Holy Spirit to fill the person. This is imperative. Pray that the person will have every "room" filled with the power and presence of the Holy Spirit. Bring forth prophetic encouragement, moving in the gifts of the Spirit that are represented in the prayer team. Release life-giving power by speaking encouraging words.

In addition, give the newly freed person some practical tools for follow-up. Seek the Lord for the ones to suggest, such as giving them an assignment to read the Bible or to make a specific, positive declaration of freedom on a regular basis.

A Prayer for Deliverance

In some cases, especially when you do not have a prayer team, an effective method can include a deliberate reading of a written prayer. First, you would lead the person through the preconditions for deliverance, such as forgiveness and repentance. If the person is not already able to identify several areas in which demonic affliction is evident, you may decide to resort to one of the inventory-type questionnaires, or you may query the person further about generational issues.

Then, using a "repeat-after-me" style, you could lead the person to make a confession of faith and then to address the darkness directly, using words such as the following ones:

"I believe Jesus Christ is the only begotten Son of God. I believe He lived a perfect life. I believe He died on the cross for my sins. I believe He was buried and rose again on the third day.

"Lord Jesus, I have repented and confessed all my sins to You. I have forgiven all those who have wronged me. I now make a conscious decision to give You complete control of my life. All that I am and all that I have, I give to You. I release everything back to You.

"I release myself by the blood of Jesus from any and all that have tried to control me. By the power of the blood of Jesus, I break every curse, hex, negative word and evil plan for my life due to my sins and the sins of my fore-parents. I renounce Satan and all his works. All that is connected with Satan and the occult I have purposed to destroy immediately. I specifically renounce (have them name the particular spirits that they feel bound or afflicted by). I declare to you evil spirit(s) that by the blood of Jesus you have been removed. You no longer have any place or power over me through the blood of Jesus. Therefore, you spirit of _____, get out in the name of Jesus Christ."

When you have a person frame his or her own prayer and then command evil spirits directly, the "hooks" by which the evil spirits have adhered to the person can be removed much more easily. The deliverance is much more effective than it would be if the person had remained passive.

Breathing Out and In

The Greek word for spirit is *pneuma*, which can also be translated as "breath." After a spirit has been commanded to leave, one option is to instruct the person to begin to blow out as a faith-filled action of expulsion. Often this will lead to a manifestation of the demon's departure (coughing, yawning, a feeling that a weight has been lifted, a scream, a screech, a hissing and so on). Although such things often occur, they do not necessarily happen. Do not be led by the nature of the manifestation, but rather by the witness of the Holy Spirit in your spirit that it is time to move on.

When you are finished, the Spirit will give a sense of relief and peace to those present. If more is needed but He tells you that this is all for now, communicate this to the person you are praying with and help them know what they should do until you get back together again.

Upon finishing a prayer of deliverance, spend some time praying for the person to be filled with the Holy Spirit (in other words, "breathing in" God's Spirit, who is the breath of life). Ask Jesus' Spirit to fill every vacancy with Himself.

Follow-Up

Talk to the person about how to walk in the new freedom that He has provided. Here are some important points to cover:

- **Keep Jesus central.** Follow Jesus in your daily decisions and model your life after His (see Luke 9:23; 2 Corinthians 5:9; 11:2–3).
- **Pray daily.** Learn to pray daily and regularly throughout the day (see Matthew 26:41; Luke 21:34–36). Do it individually (see Matthew 6:6) and with other believers (see Acts 2:42; 12:12). Peter and John prayed at regular hours (see Acts 3:1; 10:9, cf. 10:2–4).
- **Stay in the Word of God daily.** Study, meditate on, memorize and be obedient to the will of God as revealed in His written Word (see Psalm 119:9; John 8:31–32; 15:3).

- **Get baptized in water.** If this has not yet been done, get baptized in water. Baptism cuts off the legal rights of Satan to afflict and pursue, just as the Red Sea drowned Pharaoh and his army (see 1 Corinthians 10:1–2).
- **Keep short accounts.** Keep short accounts with God and man. If you fall into sin, clear it up immediately (see Matthew 5:23–25; Ephesians 4:26–27).
- **Walk in the light.** Maintain honest relationships with other committed believers.

If we [really] are living and walking in the Light, as He [Himself] is in the Light, we have [true, unbroken] fellowship with one another, and the blood of Jesus Christ His Son cleanses (removes) us from all sin and guilt [keeps us cleansed from sin in all its forms and manifestations].

1 John 1:7, AMP

- **Come under authority.** Put yourself under the God-fearing authority of Spirit-led Church leadership (see 1 Corinthians 16:15–16; 1 Thessalonians 5:12–13; Hebrews 13:17).
- **Walk in submission and community.** Humility and submission go hand in hand, submission toward authority at all levels (see James 4:6–7; 1 Peter 2:13; 5:5–8). Walk with others; we need each other. Be a committed part of the Body of Christ.
- **Walk in love and good deeds.** Walk in the opposite spirit of evil and practice the power of restitution. "Do not be overcome by evil, but overcome evil with good" (Romans 12:21).
- **Be continually led by the Holy Spirit.** "So I say, live by the Spirit, and you will not gratify the desires of the sinful nature" (Galatians 5:16, NIV).

You will never regret the effort and time that it takes to seek for deliverance, to receive and sustain it and to minister it to fellow citizens of the Kingdom of God!

> For as many as are led by the Spirit of God, these are sons of God. For you did not receive the spirit of bondage again to fear, but you received the Spirit of adoption by whom we cry out, "Abba, Father."
>
> Romans 8:14–15

PART IV

The Remedy

10

Curses: Causes and Cures

A ny book about deliverance from darkness would be incomplete without at least one chapter about curses and blessings. Breaking curses and replacing them with blessings is a vital part of becoming truly free from the power of the evil one.

The basic blessing/curses principle is encapsulated in this well-known passage of Scripture:

> This day I call heaven and earth as witnesses against you that I have set before you life and death, blessings and curses. Now choose life, so that you and your children may live and that you may love the LORD your God, listen to his voice, and hold fast to him. For the LORD is your life, and he will give you many years in the land he swore to give to your fathers, Abraham, Isaac and Jacob.
>
> Deuteronomy 30:19–20, NIV

"Choose life" is the key phrase here. Choices are involved, and they cover every aspect of life. Too often, our choices are the "default" choices, made in blind ignorance, and such choices often end up with negative results. But those of us who belong to the Lord will find no shortage of information in His Word about how to glean God's blessings by making the right choices.

I want every part of my life to be delivered from darkness, don't you? I want to find out all I can about choosing life and walking in blessings.

What Is a Curse? What Is a Blessing?

From the Word, we discover that a curse or a blessing is a statement that is made with some form of spiritual power and authority, either for evil (in the case of a curse) or for good (in the case of a blessing). Both curses and blessings set something in motion, and that motion may well continue from one generation to another.

Both curses and blessings must be "pronounced," if not audibly, then in written form or even in the form of strong mental wishes or intentions. Like ripples in a pond, their effect does not remain with one individual only, but rather expands to encompass an entire family.

Examples of blessings from the Old Testament include the following:

> Then the Angel of the LORD called to Abraham a second time out of heaven, and said: "By Myself I have sworn, says the LORD, because you have done this thing, and have not withheld your son, your only son—blessing I will bless you, and multiplying I will multiply your descendants as the stars of the heaven and as the sand which is on the seashore; and your descendants shall possess the gate of their enemies. In your seed all the nations of the earth shall be blessed, because you have obeyed My voice."
>
> Genesis 22:15–18

So he came near and kissed him; and [Isaac] smelled his clothing and blessed him and said, The scent of my son is as the
odor of a field which the Lord has blessed. And may God
give you of the dew of the heavens and of the fatness of the
earth and abundance of grain and [new] wine; let peoples
serve you and nations bow down to you; be master over your
brothers, and let your mother's sons bow down to you. Let
everyone be cursed who curses you and favored with blessings
who blesses you.

Genesis 27:27–29, AMP

The first is an example of a blessing given directly by God, in
God's words, in response to Abraham's obedience. Essentially,
it is a prophetic statement, and it was fulfilled. Abraham's seed
did multiply greatly, to the point that no one will ever be able
to calculate the number of his descendants. Looking up at the
starry sky at night, we can only marvel.

The second passage above is an example of a blessing given
by a man, Abraham's direct descendant Isaac, in God's name.
This incident well illustrates the *power* of a blessing, in view
of the fact that Isaac was fooled into giving it to his son Jacob
instead of his firstborn son, Esau—and he was not able to rescind
it even after he found out what he had done.

A blessing has "staying power"! Not only does a person choose
life when he or she chooses to line up with a divine blessing,
but the blessing itself also has a life of its own. Blessings stay
alive even when all of the original parties have died. Blessings
remain available for whoever fulfills the stated requirements.
Sad to say, curses have staying power as well.

Beyond staying power, blessings and curses also have the
power of duplication. Early in the Bible, God told Abraham,
"I will bless those who bless you, and I will curse him who
curses you" (Genesis 12:3). This is a principle that we need to

be aware of. In either case, the human initiative to bless or to curse draws down a divine blessing or curse.

Curse without a Cause

Proverbs 26:2 expresses another principle we should know: "Like the sparrow in her wandering, like the swallow in her flying, so the causeless curse does not alight" (AMP). This indicates that a curse will not afflict someone if that person does not fulfill the qualifications of a "cursee." Only when someone does fall into sin or in some way is predisposed to become a victim will a curse settle on him or her.

And according to Deuteronomy 5:9–10, which is in the middle of the Ten Commandments: "I the LORD thy God am a jealous God, visiting the iniquity of the fathers upon the children unto the third and fourth generation of them that hate me, and shewing mercy unto thousands of them that love me and keep my commandments" (KJV).

In other words, people who are God-haters are right in the path of generational curses that will run them over, generation after generation. But if they turn into God-lovers, becoming obedient to Him as their Lord, they become qualified to find release from generational curses and they can expect God to enable them to institute long-term blessings to replace the curses. We will learn more about blessings in the next chapter, which is about generational blessings.

Sources of Curses

A good part of the success in breaking curses can come with finding out what caused them in the first place. Like sin, which originates in a person's heart (see James 1:14–15), curses must be activated by human beings. They are conditional; they depend upon man-made circumstances and responses. For example, look at what Moses, speaking for God, declared:

> Cursed is the one who makes a carved or molded image, an abomination to the LORD, the work of the hands of the craftsman, and sets it up in secret.
> And all the people shall answer and say, "Amen!"
> Cursed is the one who treats his father or his mother with contempt. . . .
> Cursed is the one who moves his neighbor's landmark. . . .
> Cursed is the one who makes the blind to wander off the road. . . .
> Cursed is the one who perverts the justice due the stranger, the fatherless, and widow. . . .
> Cursed is the one who lies with his father's wife, because he has uncovered his father's bed. . . .
> Cursed is the one who lies with any kind of animal. . . .
> Cursed is the one who lies with his sister, the daughter of his father or the daughter of his mother. . . .
> Cursed is the one who lies with his mother-in-law. . . .
> Cursed is the one who attacks his neighbor secretly. . . .
> Cursed is the one who takes a bribe to slay an innocent person. . . .
> Cursed is the one who does not confirm all the words of this law by observing them.
> And all the people shall say, "Amen!"
>
> Deuteronomy 27:15–26

Moses depicted quite a range of sinful behavior that can get a person into trouble:

- Turning away from the Lord
- Dishonoring father and mother
- Changing boundary markers

- Misleading the blind (or generally hindering people who are helpless)
- Distorting justice to widows and orphans
- Committing incest, including with one's mother-in-law
- Engaging in bestiality (sexual intercourse with animals)
- Committing murder
- Conspiring like part of a hit team

And these are only some of the types of sinful behavior that will incur God's curse. He is holy, and He cannot bless a person who chooses to sin.

Remember, our behavior is a choice. But because even the best of us commit some degree of sin out of ignorance, bondage or personal willfulness, also remember that, because of Jesus, we have better recourse than the Israelites did in Moses' day.

Similar to the first element in Moses' statement above is Jeremiah's declaration: "Thus says the Lord: Cursed [with great evil] is the strong man who trusts in and relies on frail man, making weak [human] flesh his arm, and whose mind and heart turn aside from the Lord" (Jeremiah 17:5, AMP). This is an "equal opportunity" type of curse, one that can happen to any of us at any time. We had better learn how to turn away from that one by turning back to the Lord. We find a similar statement in the New Testament:

> O foolish Galatians! Who has bewitched you that you should not obey the truth, before whose eyes Jesus Christ was clearly portrayed among you as crucified? This only I want to learn from you: Did you receive the Spirit by the works of the law, or by the hearing of faith? Are you so foolish? Having begun in the Spirit, are you now being made perfect by the flesh? Have you suffered so many things in vain—if indeed it was in vain?

Therefore He who supplies the Spirit to you and works miracles among you, does He do it by the works of the law, or by the hearing of faith?

> Galatians 3:1–5

Strong language! Walking by human strength rather than by the power of the Spirit is tantamount to being "bewitched," or accursed.

Other curses that God has pronounced on people who sin in specific ways include the following:

Will a man rob or defraud God? Yet you rob and defraud Me. But you say, In what way do we rob or defraud You? [You have withheld your] tithes and offerings. You are cursed with the curse, for you are robbing Me, even this whole nation. Bring all the tithes (the whole tenth of your income) into the storehouse, that there may be food in My house, and prove Me now by it, says the Lord of hosts, if I will not open the windows of heaven for you and pour you out a blessing, that there shall not be room enough to receive it.

> Malachi 3:8–10, AMP

He asked me, "What do you see?"

I answered, "I see a flying scroll, thirty feet long and fifteen feet wide."

And he said to me, "This is the curse that is going out over the whole land; for according to what it says on one side, every thief will be banished, and according to what it says on the other, everyone who swears falsely will be banished. The LORD Almighty declares, 'I will send it out, and it will enter the house of the thief and the house of him who swears falsely by my name. It will remain in his house and destroy it, both its timbers and its stones.'"

> Zechariah 5:2–4, NIV

The former is a curse occasioned by plain old stinginess. When we fail to bring the full 10 percent of our income to the storehouse (which means to the place from which we are fed, not just anyplace), we are robbing God. The latter curse refers to a destructive curse that stays in a person's house because of stealing and perjury.

Still more curses are attached to disobedience, unfruitfulness and other sinful choices, including transgressions of preconditions that had been declared by someone in authority. For instance, after he destroyed the walls of Jericho, Joshua declared that nobody should ever rebuild those walls without doing so at the cost of his firstborn child. Could he get away with a statement like that? Well, look at the records from later years. The fact is that God did not want those walls to be rebuilt. We should not be surprised at what happened when someone tried to rebuild: "In Ahab's time, Hiel of Bethel rebuilt Jericho. He laid its foundations at the cost of his firstborn son Abiram, and he set up its gates at the cost of his youngest son Segub, in accordance with the word of the LORD spoken by Joshua son of Nun" (1 Kings 16:34, NIV).

You see, the primary reason for the release of curses is an independent, rebellious, disobedient spirit. The primary reason for blessings to be released is a submissive, obedient spirit.

Psalm 109 provides us with another example of a prophetic word that predicts accurately a curse that would happen years hence. Peter quoted it in Acts 1:20 when he said, "For it is written in the Book of Psalms: 'Let his dwelling place be desolate, and let no one live in it'; and, 'Let another take his office.'" The psalm portrays the Messiah accused by a traitor. Judas Iscariot fulfilled the words of this curse in every detail:

Appoint a wicked man over him, and let an accuser stand at his right hand. When he is judged, let him come forth guilty, and let his prayer become sin. Let his days be few; let another take his office. Let his children be fatherless and his wife a widow.

Psalm 109:6–9, NASB

The fulfillment of that curse takes my breath away.

Beyond these curses, we see scriptural curses against people who return evil for good (see Proverbs 17:13) and also Jesus' curse of the unfruitful fig tree—by extension, for any appearance of fruitfulness without any fruit (see Mark 11:12–14; 20–22). Jesus applied the unfruitfulness curse to Judaism as it was being practiced in His day, and I think that most of us recognize that the same curse could be applied to much of Christianity the way it is being practiced in our day. Both Jeremiah and James reminded people that even those who utter soulish prayers or who gossip are in danger of reaping blighted fruit (see Jeremiah 18:18; James 3:14–16).

Other Curses

Because he was her husband and therefore had authority over his wife, Jacob inadvertently cursed his beloved Rachel when he said, "The one with whom you find your gods shall not live" (Genesis 31:32, NASB). This curse was based on the portion about idols in Deuteronomy 27:15, quoted above. Rachel was the culprit; she had stolen her father's household idols. The death sentence that Jacob pronounced was fulfilled in Genesis 35:16–18 when Rachel died in childbirth.

Jacob's mother, Rebekah, had put a self-imposed curse on herself when she said, "Your curse be on me, my son" (Genesis 27:11–13, NASB). Sure enough, Jacob was not affected by the curse that should have fallen on him as a deceiver when he cheated his brother, Esau, out of their father's blessing; he went on to become a wealthy man who was blessed by God at every turn.

In the courtyard of Pontius Pilate, the Jews pronounced their own destiny when they said, "His blood shall be on us and on our children!" (Matthew 27:25, NASB). They were choosing between Jesus and Barabbas. Instead of choosing life, they chose death.

Other curses stem from unscriptural covenants: "He that sacrificeth unto any god, save unto the LORD only, he shall be utterly destroyed" (Exodus 22:20, KJV). Freemasonry would be a modern example of such a transfer of loyalty.[1] "Professional" servants of Satan such as witches, wizards and mediums convey curses to those who consult them, even if the servant of Satan does not utter a literal curse, because of God's prohibition against consulting such people (see Deuteronomy 18:10–11). Saul went to the witch of Endor, and as a direct result, he was cut off from continuing as king (see 1 Samuel 28).

In his epistles, Paul urged the members of the churches to steer clear of any kind of reviling or literal cursing (see Romans 12:14; 1 Corinthians 4:12). Putting a curse on someone else is no joke. What Balak wanted Balaam to do has tempted people at many points in history:

> Balak said: ". . . Now come and put a curse on these people, because they are too powerful for me. Perhaps then I will be able to defeat them and drive them out of the country. For I know that those you bless are blessed, and those you curse are cursed."
>
> Numbers 22:5–6, NIV

Just as Balaam did, we need to resist the temptation. As Peter put it, "Do not repay evil with evil or insult with insult, but with blessing, because to this you were called so that you may inherit a blessing" (1 Peter 3:9, NIV).

Forms of Blessings

Not surprisingly, blessings take the form of favor from God and other people, good health, fruitfulness, prosperity and victory. Moses summed up blessings in these words:

> Now it shall come to pass, if you diligently obey the voice of the LORD your God, to observe carefully all His commandments which I command you today, that the LORD your God will set you high above all nations of the earth. And all these blessings shall come upon you and overtake you, because you obey the voice of the LORD your God:
>
> Blessed shall you be in the city, and blessed shall you be in the country.
>
> Blessed shall be the fruit of your body, the produce of your ground and the increase of your herds, the increase of your cattle and the offspring of your flocks.
>
> Blessed shall be your basket and your kneading bowl.
>
> Blessed shall you be when you come in, and blessed shall you be when you go out.
>
> The LORD will cause your enemies who rise against you to be defeated before your face; they shall come out against you one way and flee before you seven ways.
>
> The LORD will command the blessing on you in your storehouses and in all to which you set your hand, and He will bless you in the land which the LORD your God is giving you.
>
> The LORD will establish you as a holy people to Himself, just as He has sworn to you, if you keep the commandments of the LORD your God and walk in His ways. Then all peoples of the earth shall see that you are called by the name of the LORD, and they shall be afraid of you. And the LORD will grant you plenty of goods, in the fruit of your body, in the increase of your livestock, and in the produce of your ground, in the land of which the LORD swore to your fathers to give you. The LORD will open to you His good treasure, the heavens, to give the rain to your land in its season, and to bless all the work of your hand.

You shall lend to many nations, but you shall not borrow. And the LORD will make you the head and not the tail; you shall be above only, and not be beneath, if you heed the commandments of the LORD your God, which I command you today, and are careful to observe them. So you shall not turn aside from any of the words which I command you this day, to the right or the left, to go after other gods to serve them.

Deuteronomy 28:1–14

In the next chapter, you will be able to learn more about accepting and completing the blessings that God wants to give you.

Review of Curses

Deuteronomy 28 goes on to give a summary of the various forms that curses can take. The list serves as a counterpoint to the types of blessings enumerated at the beginning of that chapter. It is a long list, odious to read, and it can be summed up in a few key words. If you choose to transgress God's stated will, you can expect to reap humiliation, mental and physical sickness, family breakdown, poverty, defeat, oppression and failure—in short, God's disfavor (see Deuteronomy 28:15–68).

Although the culture has changed over the centuries, the results of curses are the same:

- Mental and emotional breakdown
- Repeated or chronic sickness (especially when there is no clear medical reason)
- Repeated miscarriage and related female problems
- Breakdown of family, resulting in alienation
- Continual financial insufficiency (especially where income appears to be sufficient)

- Repeated accidents, being accident-prone
- Family history of suicides or unnatural deaths

From Moses' time to the present, we can identify twelve possible causes for curses:

1. Idolatry, false gods, the occult
2. Dishonoring parents
3. Illicit or unnatural sex
4. Injustice to the weak or helpless
5. Trusting in the "arm of flesh"
6. Stealing or perjury
7. Withholding tithes
8. Pronouncements made by a person in relational authority
9. Pronouncements made by a person about him-/herself (self-imposed curses)
10. Pronouncements made by people who represent Satan (witch doctors, etc.)
11. Gossip and other utterances spoken with a wrong attitude, including soulish prayers that are not inspired by the Holy Spirit
12. Unscriptural covenants

We cannot pretend that the cause-and-effect of curses and blessings does not exist. The smart thing to do is to ask the Holy Spirit to help you take a good hard look at your own life. Where you see circumstances that could represent the result of curses, ask Him to give you further revelation. Then undo the curse in His name and as He leads, with help from someone else if needed.

In my own life I can testify to the power of both blessings and curses and also to the connection of curses with demonic strongholds. Without going into too much detail in a public venue, I can say that my upbringing included some harmful influences and those influences left a strong residue that could definitely be termed curses. My life was characterized by a fear of retribution, fear of rejection, fear of authority and more. Through God's grace and by applying His truth in my life, I began to make choices that led to blessings.

Sometimes the transfer from darkness to light is very obvious and the pathway is traceable. For example, my late wife was named Michal after David's wife Michal in the Bible. As you know, David's wife Michal was cursed with barrenness because she had mocked David for dancing before the Lord (see 2 Samuel 6:14–23). Likely because of the association with her name, my wife, too, was barren—at first. We broke the curse in the name of Jesus, and my wife became fruitful, giving birth to four wonderful children in succession, two girls and two boys.

Your Legal and Experiential Rights

To walk free of curses in your own life (and to convert them to blessings), you must start by understanding the source of good and evil, God Himself. "Every good thing given and every perfect gift is from above, coming down from the Father of lights, with whom there is no variation or shifting shadow" (James 1:17, NASB). We have one source for every good thing: God. We have one channel for His blessings: Jesus Christ. We have one basis for appropriating His blessings: the cross. And we have one means of appropriating His blessings: faith.

By a divine exchange, Jesus Christ has redeemed us from the curse of the Law. Isaiah prophesied it and Jesus fulfilled His word: "All we like sheep have gone astray; we have turned, every one, to his own way; and the LORD has laid on Him the iniquity of us all" (Isaiah 53:6). Paul articulated it in one of His New Testament letters:

Christ redeemed us from the curse of the Law, having become a
curse for us—for it is written, "Cursed is everyone who hangs on
a tree"—in order that in Christ Jesus the blessing of Abraham
might come to the Gentiles, so that we would receive the promise
of the Spirit through faith.

Galatians 3:13–14, NASB

The cross of Jesus is the gateway between curses and blessings.
But believers do not pass through that gateway automatically.
As has always been the case, we take possession of our promised
land by listening and obeying. The long chapter in Deuteronomy
that details blessings and curses begins with these words:

If you will *listen* diligently to the voice of the Lord your God,
being watchful to *do all His commandments* which I command
you this day, the Lord your God will set you high above all the
nations of the earth. And all these blessings shall come upon you
and overtake you *if you heed* the voice of the Lord your God.

Deuteronomy 28:1–2, AMP, emphasis added
(See also Deuteronomy 28:15; Exodus 15:26)

It is one thing to have legal rights, and it is another thing to
possess experiential enjoyment of those rights. The right to be
free from curses is legally yours from the moment you declared
your allegiance to Jesus. But if you just stand in front of your
house and declare "I'm blessed! I'm blessed! I'm blessed!" without listening to God and without obeying what you hear Him
say, your situation will remain unchanged for a long time.

You can inherit a fortune, but there is a process involved in
receiving it. You will not get it if you do not act. Even if you
do act, someone might contest your right. In the case of your
heavenly inheritance, Jesus Christ is your legal advocate with
the Father (see 1 John 2:1–2). Your inheritance will be released
with His help.

After the children of Israel had wandered for forty years, God showed them the Promised Land again (see Joshua 1:2–4). This time would be different, because this time they would act. Instead of drawing back in fear, this time they would be able to possess that territory. Under Joshua's leadership, they crossed the Jordan and conquered Jericho. Technically, the land had been theirs all along, because God had delivered it to them. Now it could be theirs experientially.

How to Walk through the Gateway

Again in review, God has provided us with definite steps that will take us to the promised land of milk and honey (blessings), where we can be free from curses. The seven basic steps involve four key verbs: Recognize, Repent, Renounce and Resist:

1. Establish a clear scriptural basis.[2]
2. Confess your faith in Christ.[3]
3. Commit yourself to obedience.[4]
4. Confess any known sins committed by your ancestors or you yourself.[5]
5. Forgive.[6]
6. Renounce all contact with the occult.[7]
7. Release yourself from curses and the hold of the devil, in the name of Jesus.[8]

You can continue to walk in freedom by staying close to the Lord, listening to His Spirit and obeying what He tells you to do. Make every effort to cooperate with Him as he brings you out of darkness and into His marvelous light. "You are a chosen race, a royal priesthood, a holy nation, a people for God's own possession, so that you may proclaim the excellencies of Him who has called you out of darkness into His marvelous light" (1 Peter 2:9, NASB).

Prayers of Release and Thanksgiving

If you wish, you can use these prayers of release from the powers of darkness:

Prayer of Release (Offered for Oneself)

Dear Father, I believe that Jesus Christ is the Son of God and that He is the only way to God, that on the cross He died for my sins, that He rose again from the dead, and that on the cross He was made a curse so that I might be redeemed and receive Your blessing.

I trust You now for mercy and forgiveness and I commit myself from now on by Your grace to follow and obey You. I ask You to forgive and blot out any sins committed by me or by my ancestors that exposed me to a curse (at this point name any specific sins of which you are aware).

If people have harmed me or wronged me, I forgive them, as I would have God forgive me (name those people).

I renounce all contact with Satan, occult practices and unscriptural secret societies (name the specific practices or secret societies with which you or your parents, grandparents or other close relatives were involved). If I own any objects that link me to these things, reveal them to me. I promise to destroy them.

With the authority You have given me as a child of God, I release myself from every curse that has ever come upon me or affected me in any way, in the name of Jesus. Amen.

Prayer of Release (Offered by One Ministering)

Gracious Father, I thank You that You allowed Jesus, on the cross, to become a curse that we, through Him, might be redeemed from the curse. I thank You for those who have prayed this prayer in faith, meeting every condition. I break every satanic power over their lives. I revoke every curse. Lord Jesus, I claim full release for them now, as they are thanking You. I declare that Satan is a defeated enemy, that all his claims have been cancelled by the shed blood of Jesus. I pronounce them free in the name of Jesus. I declare that Satan's authority is revoked and cancelled forever, in the name of Jesus. Amen!

11

Generational Blessings

The power of a blessing is much greater than the power of a curse. In fact, a blessing can overcome a curse outright. Sometimes you do not even have to address evil spirits or generational curses, because the power of the blessing will do it for you. I learned this experientially years ago and I have proved it many times since.

At that time, I had been having many dreams in which I saw corporate declarations of blessing followed by light being released into and over crowds of people, who were healed without anyone touching them.

I had the dream so many times; I was primed for action when I went to Southeast Asia to minister. I was preaching in an Anglican church in Bangkok, Thailand, during the daytime and ministering in open renewal meetings in the YMCA at night. My topic was "Curses," and I had been doing systematic teaching that was being translated for the sake of the people, who did not know English. We had been dealing with a lot of curses that had been placed on people through much Buddhist activity.

Finishing up one session, instead of confronting the evil one as expected, I started proclaiming blessings in the name of Jesus, declaring the power of the blessing. I declared that the light was present, the light would come and the light would have an effect on the people. Most of my words were not being translated; I was just speaking blessings directly in English.

A lady who was paralyzed on one side of her body was sitting in those meetings. When she walked, she dragged one leg and one of her arms was hanging down. She had gone through every test imaginable. She was scheduled for one more MRI to try to find the source of the paralysis. I had not noticed her when she came in and I did not know anything about her.

As I began to directly address the power of blessing, I could feel the power surge in the room. Later, she said it was as if a bolt of electric energy hit her body. No one had laid hands on her.

That night in the open meetings, this woman was up in front of everybody, dancing all over the place. People were excited, because they knew who she was. That is when I found out what had happened earlier; her paralysis had disappeared. There she was—dancing, fully healed and fully restored, a living illustration of the power of the blessing operating in the opposite spirit of cursing.

What Is a Blessing?

To find a clear definition, I examined various dictionary sources for the noun "blessing," which can mean "a prayer or solemn wish imploring happiness upon another; a benediction; the act of pronouncing a benediction or blessing; that which promotes prosperity and welfare." Similarly, I looked at various dictionary sources for the verb "to bless," which can be defined as "to invoke the divine favor on; to bestow happiness, prosperity or good things of all kinds; to make a pronouncement holy;

to consecrate; to glorify for the benefits received; to extol for excellencies."

Hebrew-speakers use the word *berakah* for "blessing." It means "benediction" (the act of invoking a blessing) and for us it brings to mind the traditional benediction of a congregation at the end of a church liturgy. The word is used almost seventy times in the Old Testament; here it is in the familiar introductory words of Psalm 133:

> Behold, how good and how pleasant it is for brethren to dwell together in unity! It is like the precious ointment upon the head, that ran down upon the beard, even Aaron's beard: that went down to the skirts of his garments; as the dew of Hermon, and as the dew that descended upon the mountains of Zion: for there the LORD commanded the *blessing*, even life for evermore.
>
> Psalm 133:1–3, KJV, emphasis added

The word *berakah* comes from the root word *barak*, which means "to kneel" and which by implication means "to bless." The word is used throughout the Hebrew Scriptures: "*Bless* the LORD, O house of Israel: *bless* the LORD, O house of Aaron: *bless* the LORD, O house of Levi: ye that fear the LORD, *bless* the LORD" (Psalm 135:19–20, KJV, emphasis added).

My working definition of the word *blessing* is this: "A blessing is a word spoken for good that carries spiritual power and authority and that sets in motion something that will probably go on from generation to generation." My definition is based on the biblical nature of a blessing (or a curse), as I outlined it in the previous chapter. Both curses and blessings carry great power. To do so, they must be pronounced audibly or written down, yet even when they come in the form of strong mental wishes or intentions, they spread like ripples in a pond, encompassing an entire family over multiple generations.

In chapter 10, I quoted Genesis 22:15–18 and Genesis 27:27–29 as examples of Old Testament blessings. I also quoted Deuteronomy 28:1–14, with its long list of specific blessings. In every case, the conditions surrounding blessings fall into several categories:

1. A blessing can be for an individual (personal) or for a group (corporate).
2. A blessing, like the gifts of God (see Romans 11:29) cannot be rescinded or taken back.
3. A blessing pronounced by a father or someone in authority has extra significance.
4. Someone who listens to the Lord and obeys Him is in a good position to receive blessings.
5. Scriptural blessings (see Deuteronomy 28:1–14) include:
   • Encouragement
   • Productivity and fruitfulness
   • Health
   • Prosperity
   • Victory
   • God's favor

God spoke to Abraham and blessed him with these words:

> I will make you a great nation,
>> And I will bless you,
>> And make your name great;
>> And so you shall be a blessing;
> And I will bless those who bless you,
>> And the one who curses you I will curse
>> And in you all the families of the earth will be
>> blessed.
>
> Genesis 12:2–3, NASB

This is an amazing and powerful blessing. And yet Jesus has brought us *greater* blessings than these Old Testament blessings. The writer of the book of Hebrews details all of the blessings and privileges of the priests and the Law, and then he goes on to write, "But the ministry Jesus has received is as superior to theirs as the covenant of which he is mediator is superior to the old one, and it is founded on better promises" (Hebrews 8:6, NIV).

Jesus has brought to earth all of the blessings of heaven, and He has added them to the blessings of the Hebraic covenant. Like the blazing sun superseding the shadows of the night, His blessings can supersede the curses of darkness.

Wrestling for a Blessing

After obtaining his father Isaac's blessing dishonestly (essentially stealing Esau's blessing), Jacob fled from home. Living with his uncle Laban in Haran, he became a wealthy man. After many years, he gathered up his wives and children, servants, flocks and herds—and his courage—and headed back to "face the music" with his aggrieved brother. Just before he got there:

> [Jacob] took his two wives, his two women servants, and his eleven sons and passed over the ford [of the] Jabbok. And he took them and sent them across the brook; also he sent over all that he had.
>
> And Jacob was left alone, and a Man wrestled with him until daybreak. And when [the Man] saw that He did not prevail against [Jacob], He touched the hollow of his thigh; and Jacob's thigh was put out of joint as he wrestled with Him.
>
> Then He said, Let Me go, for day is breaking. But [Jacob] said, *I will not let You go unless You declare a blessing upon me.*
>
> [The Man] asked him, What is your name? And [in shock of realization, whispering] he said, Jacob [supplanter, schemer,

trickster, swindler]! And He said, your name shall be called no more Jacob [supplanter], but Israel [contender with God]; for you have contended and have power with God and with men and have prevailed.

Then Jacob asked Him, Tell me, I pray You, what [in contrast] is Your name? But He said, Why is it that you ask My name? And *[the Angel of God declared] a blessing on [Jacob] there.*

Genesis 32:22–29, AMP, emphasis added

This story illustrates several key features of blessings. One is simply the fact that sometimes you have to wrestle with God so that you can receive blessings. Although God wants to give them to you, blessings do not always come easily or automatically.

Several other highlights flow from that one:

1. *Striving or wrestling with God for a blessing will result in your nature being changed.* This may be God's primary goal; He wants your identity to change. In Jacob's case the angel of the Lord renamed him from "Jacob," which connoted someone who stepped into another person's identity by using deception, to "Israel," which means "God strives" or "God prevails." His nature had been changed from someone who obtained victory dishonestly to someone who fought tirelessly and honestly.

2. *Not only was his name changed, but his character was also changed.* Jacob would not let God's angel go until he had received the full portion of his inheritance. Perseverance is a vital quality in the Kingdom of God (see Luke 21:19; James 1:12; 2 Peter 1:5–8). So is assertiveness. Although much of the Church has been lulled into passivity, yet God is a warrior (see Exodus 15:3).

3. *Wrestling for and receiving the blessing is a dual process.* Winning involves being like a holy, tenacious bulldog that

will not let go. You need to be passionate and aggressive for God's purposes. Winning also involves displacing darkness with light, supplanting and negating the enemy's plans with blessing.

You and the Blessing

Many of us grew up in fine families, but our parents did not know about the power of blessing their children. As a consequence, we have struggled for our whole lives to obtain a blessing that would establish us as beloved and secure children who belong ultimately to God. Every avenue of satisfaction that we have tried has been a dead end.

When Esau recognized that he had lost his father's blessing forever, he cried out in anguish, "Bless me—me too, my father!" (Genesis 27:34, NIV). This is the cry of every heart.

Gary Smalley and John Trent wrote a book called *The Blessing*, in which they presented five distinct expressions of effective blessings.[1]

Meaningful Touch

Touch imparts and releases life, warmth, compassion and blessing. Paul told the Romans that he wanted to be *with* them in order to impart a blessing to them (see Romans 1:11). Parents impart blessings to their children by holding them. Friends and relatives bless each other through hugs and meaningful touching.

The Hebrew term *massa´* means "burden" or "load," and it is used with reference to carrying the burden of the Lord's heart, with prophetic overtones. Sometimes the word is translated "oracle." When somebody carries a blessing to another person, they are conveyers of God's care, transmitting the love of His heart.

173

A Spoken Word

Along with meaningful touch, words convey blessings in an especially powerful way. Obviously prophetic in nature, spoken blessings tap into God's thoughts and feelings.

I once attended a church that handled their children's dedication service in a very special way. Instead of simply having all the parents bring their children to the front for a quick word of prayer, the church would prepare specific words of blessing beforehand. They would do a word study on the meaning of the name of each child and write it out, then give it to the child's family as a gift. Each child was made significant in a personal way.

Attaching High Value to the One Being Blessed

Your words plus meaningful touch are not a blessing unless you are attaching high value to the person you are blessing. Just as the church did at their children's dedications, you are personalizing the act of blessing. You are not pasting a "one-size-fits-all" blessing onto a faceless individual. If you are addressing a problem, you are looking beyond diagnosing it, endeavoring to supply a prescription from the heart of God for the remedy. You are giving honor as you speak life-giving words, words that make it clear you (and God) consider the person valuable. "We need you." "You are valuable for the purposes of God."

Picturing a Special Future

Blessings are forward-looking. Blessings help propel people into their destiny. Along with attaching high value to the person in the present, you are giving them a glimpse of favor for the future. Whether your words of blessing are spot-on specific or more general, the recipient will be able to envision the future with hope and joy. It is really true to say, "God has a wonderful plan for your life!"

An Active Commitment

To see a blessing fulfilled, you (the one giving the blessing) need to "put legs under it." A word of blessing may wither, even if it was delivered perfectly, without any subsequent follow-up. Your involvement in the life of the other person may range from prayer to intensive practical help. You not only help a person envision the future, you ask God for the ability to empower and equip the person to fulfill their vision. You make a commitment and you follow through with it.

About ten years ago, a trusted prophet told me and my family that she saw us owning land, and that on that property would be horses. This would be a gift to our children to let them know that God loved them and had remembered their dreams (one of them in particular had yearned for a horse). It would also be a reward to them for their sacrifice of yielding their parents to God for His purposes.

When I heard this word, I did not know what to do with it. It seemed like a big stretch. We certainly did not have the money to buy a piece of property, and I did not think we would have the funds to care for horses, either. Then someone offered us a white Arabian mare—for free. Mercifully, when that happened my logic was turned off, and I accepted the gift. I received the blessing on behalf of my family.

Bolstered by some other "coincidences," I began to make an active commitment to this word of blessing. Someone had offered a word of blessing and now I had to make room for it, in a practical and seemingly impossible way, by acquiring some land and providing support for this horse and likely more horses. The outcome would have to be supernatural, but we would have to do something with what we knew.

We located a beautiful piece of property that was not even for sale and we felt that we should claim it. We did not have the money, not even close to enough money. Then suddenly, we got a windfall. Along with that, the value of the property fell at the same time that the owner decided to put it on the market. It was a miraculous provision. We bought the property and moved ourselves and our horse to it. I have the property to this day, with more horses. I am still actively committed to this particular word of blessing!

Powerful, Obtainable Blessings

You may say, "My parents never spoke words of blessing to me. Nobody has ever given me any prophetic words. I don't know what my blessings are."

I am here to tell you that you have plenty of blessings, if you know where to look for them. Here are a few places to look:

Biblical Promises

Read and study your Bible and search out God's promises for your life. You can claim every one of the promises in the Good Book as a personal promise to you. Even if you do not know about any earthly family blessings, you can lay hold of the blessings of Abba Daddy because you are part of His family. Ask the Holy Spirit to bring the Word alive for you in this way.

Family Genealogy

Ask the Lord to help you look redemptively at your family history. What does your last name mean? Can you name a strength in your family heritage? How could you describe this strength in terms of a family blessing so you can claim it for yourself and also pass it on?

I had an unusual experience in this regard. My family name is Goll, which is German. On my first visit to Germany, I had a vision of a man with a jacket and a hat on, bent over, hoeing in a field. He straightened up, looked into my eyes and said, "You will be the answer to our prayers." This baffled me. My father had grown up in an abusive home, and when I thought about the Goll side of my family, all I could identify was generational abuse. I did not know what to do with the vision.

A number of years later, I was ministering in a church in the Baltimore area that is mostly African American. A person came up to me and said, "I want to thank you that your Goll ancestors were the ones who brought the Gospel to my people."

Mystified, I asked, "Where did you come from?" Liberia—and this person's last name was Goll! Apparently many years before, a German missionary had come to Liberia to start an orphanage. Not only did he operate an orphanage, but he had also *adopted* all of the orphans, giving the children his own last name—which was Goll. Now there is a whole tribe of black Golls in Liberia.

That is how I found out that my name had a highly redemptive strength that had been a great blessing to others. It was as if one generation (my father's) had skipped a righteous blessing, and yet it had survived so that it could be picked up by the next generation (mine). Once I put the puzzle pieces together, a clearer picture emerged and I could lay hold of the blessing of my earthly family of origin.

Ethnic Group

What is your ethnic or national background? Spanish, French, Italian, African, German . . . ? God has bestowed a redemptive gift on each ethnic grouping, a redeeming national trait.

So someone like me, who is half German, can claim the blessing of the redeeming German quality—which is being a warrior.

Think about it; for good or for bad, Germans tend to be warriors. So if you have German lineage, you can obtain the warrior blessing and it will make you able to fight for the Kingdom of God. "From the days of John the Baptist until now the kingdom of heaven suffereth violence, and the violent take it by force" (Matthew 11:12, KJV).

If you have English ancestors, you can look for an anointing that comes from that bloodline heritage. The English are teachers and missionaries and they have a teacher anointing. They are exporters of the Word. This is a fascinating subject and a rich source of personalized blessings.

Church Promises

What is your denominational background? Maybe you do not have any, but if you do, see if you can identify it. Sometimes it matches your ethnic background. You can call forth the fire of John Wesley (Methodist), the purity of the Quakers, the boldness of the Pentecostals or the evangelistic anointing of the Baptists.

My own background is heavily Methodist, and the Methodists are famous for their circuit riders. Their preachers traveled far and wide, spreading a passionate response to the Good News. John Wesley said, "The world is my parish." One day I had a revelation. *What in the world am I? I cannot sit still. I get bored if I have to stay in one place too long. I am a Holy Ghost circuit rider!* Instead of riding my horse from one place to another, I hop airplanes.

Geographic—City, State, Region

Take note of your current town or city, your state or province and other regional identifiers. Do you know anything about the spiritual history of your area? Do you know of any revivals?

Conflicts? Regional characteristics? Can you figure out what God's redemptive purpose might be? Do not look only at what the powers of darkness have destroyed or how the territorial spirits of darkness hold your region in bondage; look for the positive features.

For example, I live in the Nashville area, which is known as Music City, USA. Much of the music exalts sinful behavior. However, part of the redemptive gift of God over this region is education and publishing. Increasingly, Christian music and teaching are being published here. In fact, more Christian books and Bibles are now published in Nashville than in any city in the world, and more Christian music is recorded and distributed here than anyplace else on the planet. When I moved here, I tapped into that blessing myself, publishing and distributing more teaching materials than I ever thought possible.

Another connection: A Methodist named E. M. Bounds, who wrote many volumes about prayer, moved from Missouri to Nashville around the time of the Civil War. Specifically, he moved to Franklin, which is exactly where I live. I can identify with E. M. Bounds. I am a Methodist from Missouri (both of us are north Missourians), and I came to Franklin to help lead prayer at a time of war. For me, the blessing takes the form of laying hold of his mantle of prayer.

What Is in a Name?

Consider your given name. Do you know what it means? Why did your parents bestow it on you? After a little research, you can call forth the redemptive characteristics of your first and middle names.

For example, my middle name is Wayne and that was also my father's middle name. It means "wagon-builder" or "burden-bearer"; a wagon carries cargo from one place to the next. My father owned a lumberyard and carpentry was his trade. I am not a carpenter, but I am the son of a carpenter and I can redeem my name by being a builder in the Kingdom of God, one who carries cargo and burdens from place to place. One of my sons is named Justin Wayne and, redemptively speaking, he carries justice from one place of darkness to a place of redemption.

Prophetic Words

Has God spoken promises directly to you and your family? What destiny or blessing does He want you to fulfill? Even if you do not recollect any blessings from God that have been vocalized in your hearing, you can ask Him to make it possible for you to receive prophetic input now.

Since you are suffering from a shortage of His Word, you can pray for a clear and direct word from God. To your situation, you can apply Paul's advice about interpretation of tongues:

> Therefore let one who speaks in a tongue pray that he may interpret. . . . I will pray with the spirit and I will pray with the mind also; I will sing with the spirit and I will sing with the mind also. Otherwise if you bless in the spirit only, how will the one who fills the place of the ungifted say the "Amen" at your giving of thanks, since he does not know what you are saying?
>
> 1 Corinthians 14:13, 15–16, NASB

You can bless yourself or others in the Spirit, and then, enabled by the Spirit, you can interpret the blessing. With God's help, you can bless others in Spirit and in truth. You are blessed to be a blessing. First you obtain and proclaim deliverance from darkness, then you step into the light—and after that, nothing can stop you from switching on the light of blessing for your family, your church, your neighbors and for anyone anywhere you go.

If nobody else is blessing you, stand in front of a mirror and prophesy a blessing over yourself. I have done that more than once. Tap into the living water that is flowing out of your innermost being (see John 7:38) and speak the word of God over your own life.

In benediction, receive as blessings the following prayers from the Bible:

> Praise the LORD, O my soul;
>> all my inmost being, praise his holy name.
> Praise the LORD, O my soul,
>> and forget not all his benefits—
> who forgives all your sins
>> and heals all your diseases,
> who redeems your life from the pit
>> and crowns you with love and compassion,
> who satisfies your desires with good things
>> so that your youth is renewed like the eagle's.
>
> Psalm 103:1–5, NIV

> The LORD bless you, and keep you;
> The LORD make His face shine on you,
>> And be gracious to you;
> The LORD lift up His countenance on you,
>> And give you peace.
>
> Numbers 6:24–26, NASB

12

Deliverance Made Easy

Achieving deliverance from darkness can definitely be a battle, but by grace complete victory belongs to you, provided that you are prepared, well-clothed and well-armed with God's every provision (see Ephesians 6:11–18). In fact, most of your success in battle lies in the preparation. The actual engagement of deliverance does not have to be messy or difficult at all. Believe it or not, deliverance can be easy! Before I proceed to support that statement, let me remind you of what deliverance consists of.

The Gospel of Deliverance

Jesus came to destroy the works of the devil (see 1 John 3:8). Anointed "with the Holy Spirit and with power . . . He went about doing good and healing all who were oppressed by the devil" (Acts 10:38, NASB). By healing people and casting out demons, He was bringing in the Kingdom (see Matthew 12:28).

You and I, as members of His Body here on earth, carry on with the same purposes as He did when He quoted Isaiah 61:1 in the synagogue at Nazareth:

> The Spirit of the Lord is upon Me,
>> because He anointed Me to preach the gospel to the poor.
>
> He has sent Me to proclaim release to the captives,
> and recovery of sight to the blind,
> to set free those who are oppressed,
> to proclaim the favorable year of the LORD.
>
> Luke 4:18–19, NASB

The Gospel of the Kingdom is a message of deliverance. It is a message of freedom and cleansing. As Kingdom people, we walk out of darkness and into liberty and light as we pray, "Search me, O God, and know my heart: try me, and know my thoughts: and see if there be any wicked way in me, and lead me in the way everlasting" (Psalm 139:23–24, KJV).

As Kingdom people, we combat invisible powers of darkness that masquerade as ordinary earthly entanglements. "For we are not wrestling with flesh and blood [contending only with physical opponents], but against the despotisms, against the powers, against [the master spirits who are] the world rulers of this present darkness, against the spirit forces of wickedness in the heavenly (supernatural) sphere" (Ephesians 6:12, AMP).

These spirit beings may be largely invisible to our earthly eyes, but they are very real. They exhibit various personality traits such as emotions (see James 2:19), knowledge (see Mark 1:24) and a definite willfulness (see Matthew 12:43–45). When they encounter the power of Jesus, the powers of darkness recognize that they must leave (review the "case studies" from the gospels and Acts of the Apostles such as Mark 1:21–28, 5:1–20, 9:14–29 and Acts 16:16–18).

The Father's Love

The power of Jesus comes from the extraordinary love of our Father. Greater than any darkness is the light of our all-loving Father God, the One who sent His best to us—His only Son, Jesus. His amazing Spirit dwells in the hearts of every believer, thus enabling each one of us to carry on the supernatural work that Jesus did and still does today.

The Father's love is enormously important in the ministry of deliverance and, quite frankly, it is the missing key from many presentations about deliverance. If we can create a culture based on the revelation of the loving fatherhood of God, we will not need to wrestle so long and so hard anymore. What do I mean by a "revelation of the loving fatherhood of God"?

Lessons from My Personal Journey

Like many other people, I came to know Jesus at an early age. I loved Him; He was my friend; I was very comfortable with Him. Then I experienced the infilling of His Holy Spirit and I became accustomed to His contagious presence, too. However, I did not really know the merciful love of my Father God.

Naturally, I was familiar with the words that came from heaven when Jesus was baptized: "This is My Son, in whom I am well pleased" (see Matthew 3:17; Mark 1:11; Luke 3:22). Growing up in a Protestant church, I prayed the Lord's Prayer often, and I knew that Jesus had taught His disciples to pray "Our Father . . ." (see Matthew 6:9–13; Luke 11:2–4). I knew that Jesus had said, "I am the way, the truth, and the life. No one comes to the Father except through Me" (John 14:6).

In many ways, I already knew that Jesus wanted to introduce me to His Father and to make me fully His son. But I could not embrace it—there were hindrances to intimacy for sure. So the Holy Spirit had to make a way for me to experientially know the

Father's love. Without His direct help, I would have continued to think of God the Father as aloof and even stern—as my own earthly father had been much of my life.

My father grew up in rural Missouri during the Depression, the eldest of seven children. His father kicked him out of the house when he was only twelve years old, so he never had more than a sixth-grade education. I cannot imagine the pain he went through raising himself, but somehow he made it and later joined the army, served in World War II and then married my dear mom. Growing up, I did have a few special connection times with my dad and I knew he cared for me, but I also lived in dread and fear of him—for several good reasons. I never experienced unconditional love; instead, I felt ignored or tolerated at best. Insecure and with a rejection complex, I went to college, surrendered freshly to Jesus and to my call to ministry. I then met the amazing Michal Ann Willard, married her and eventually started raising our own family. I preached about the love of Jesus and I knew it was real. I even helped others overcome their wounds of rejection. I learned how to defeat the devil with the Word and all of the other weapons of the Spirit. All the weapons, that is, except one—the mightiest weapon of all, security in the love of the Father.

Later in this chapter, I will tell you how the Lord made it possible for me to receive a blessing from my earthly father so that I could step freely into the glorious light of freedom as a beloved son of my heavenly Father. But first I want to share with you more about the richness of the Father's love. Like me, you need to know what it means to belong to Him. If you are His, He is yours!

You Are Mine

The Father created you and He loves you so very much that He sent His Son, Jesus, to open the way to heaven for you. Your

Father did not kick you out of His house when you were a child. Even if you have felt far from Him, He has always been holding out His arms to you.[1]

He chose to create you. In fact, He had you in mind at the Creation.[2] You are not an afterthought or a mistake; He has even planned the length of your life.[3] Although you may not know Him, He knows every detail about you.[4] He says, "I know when you sit down and when you rise up. I am familiar with all your ways."[5] Amazingly, your Father knows the exact number of hairs on your head.[6]

Even before you were conceived on earth, your heavenly Papa knew you.[7] He is the One who knit you together in your mother's womb with amazing precision.[8] With perfect timing, He caused you to be born into your particular family, and He planned where you would grow up.[9] He has been orchestrating everything. In other words, you are more His child than you are even a child of your earthly mother and father.[10] Your "family resemblance" is remarkable.[11]

Because He is your true Father, He wants to lavish His love on you.[12] It may seem too good to be true, but He is the perfect Father,[13] not the distant and angry Father-God that people have misbelieved Him to be.[14] Unlike your earthly father, your true Father can provide everything you will ever need, because He owns *everything*.[15] Your heavenly Father wants to establish you in the security of His loving provision.[16]

Your Father is as much your own Father as He is the Father of Jesus, His beloved Son.[17] Both He and your brother Jesus love you with an everlasting, inexhaustible love, and they will never stop doing good to you.[18] Your Father is excited about His plans for your future, because He considers you His treasure.[19] He loves to surprise you with marvelous gifts.[20]

Does this make you want to open your heart to your Father in a new way? *Daddy, Abba, Papa?* He put those desires into your heart, you know.[21] He is whispering to you, "Seek Me with all your heart and you will find me; delight in Me and I will delight you by giving you the desires of your heart."[22] Did you realize that He is willing and able to do more for you than you could possibly imagine?[23] He welcomes you. He goes way beyond tolerating you—He celebrates you!

Who would think that His thoughts toward you (toward just you, personally!) would be so numerous that nobody can count them?[24] Hard as it is to believe, your Father actually rejoices over you—with singing![25] Your Father is your greatest cheerleader. He can supply you with encouragement, vigor and confidence every day of your life.[26] He sent Jesus (who is the exact representation of His being) to show you that He is *for* you, never against you.[27] Jesus' Father is the same as your Father, and Jesus' death was the ultimate expression of the Father's desire to have you near.[28]

Your Father knows how hard life can become. He longs to comfort you, both here and now, on earth, and later in heaven.[29] He wants you to know that when you are brokenhearted, He will pick you up like an injured, weak lamb. He will carry you close to His heart.[30] If you are that close to Him, nothing will ever be able to separate you from His love—no impending threat is ever going to be greater than His love.[31] His love is unquenchable, and His affection is directed toward *you*![32] Look up! He is waiting for your response.[33]

Know the One You Belong To

When you come into a true revelation of the Father's love for you, you will rise to a new level of freedom. The hooks of rejection and fear will be removed from your life, and you will be able to move beyond mere techniques and information. That is when deliverance will become easy. After all, as Jesus said, "My yoke is easy, and my burden is light" (Matthew 11:30, KJV). He carries you. He takes care of everything.

Correct deliverance procedures and awe-inspiring worship are always helpful, but the most important thing is knowing the One you belong to. When you are being carried by your Daddy, you are no longer facing the darkness on your own. No longer an abandoned orphan, you become a confident son or daughter. Even if you do not know all of the A-B-C-D-X-Y-Zs of His plan for your life, you have the security and identity that you need to allow your life-purpose to play out. Your Daddy is 100 percent *for* you! A revelation of the Father's love for you is the *summum bonum*, which is Latin for "the highest good, from which all other good things are derived"—including deliverance from every form of darkness.

Blocks to the Father's Love

"Okay," you may be saying. "I understand the Father's love with my mind. But I would not say that deliverance is easy. My heart is somewhere else, and I don't know what to do about it."

Please allow me to remind you of a few things, starting with the all-essential element of forgiveness. Do a "forgiveness check." Forgiveness is the prerequisite to freedom (see Matthew 18:21–35). Harboring even a smidgen of unforgiveness in your heart will cloud your vision and interfere with your freedom.

Since we are focusing on receiving a revelation of the Father's love, you might also want to check for unhealthy emotional dependencies on other people, or "soul ties." Soul ties provide a form of nurture and security that can dull your awareness of your need for the Father's love. Ask the Lord to show you any emotional or soul ties that may be getting in the way, and then break them off in Jesus' name. When you have a soul tie, you can expect to find several of the following characteristics in your daily life: [34]

1. Jealousy, possessiveness, exclusivity; viewing other people as a threat to a relationship
2. Irrational anger or depression when the other person withdraws slightly
3. Loss of interest in other friendships
4. Preoccupation with the other person's appearance, personality problems and interest
5. Inability to see the other person's faults realistically
6. Possible romantic and sexual feelings that lead to fantasizing and inappropriate expressions of affection
7. Stagnation and limitation on personal growth
8. Selfish lack of desire to see the other person reach his or her full potential in God
9. Inability to allow God to meet your need for love and security

Unconfessed sin in general is closely related to soul ties (see 1 Corinthians 6:15–20). Confessing sin implies walking in the light of the Father's love rather than hiding in the shadows of fear and rejection:

> This is the message we have heard from him and declare to you: God is light; in him there is no darkness at all. If we claim to have fellowship with him yet walk in the darkness, we lie and do not live by the truth. But if we walk in the light, as he is in the light, we have fellowship with one another, and the blood of Jesus, his Son, purifies us from all sin.
>
> 1 John 1:5–7, NIV

Walking in the light of the Father's love makes it possible for you to move in the opposite spirit of the fears and other bondages that may have blocked you from deliverance. His perfect love casts out every form of fear (see 1 John 4:18). His love opens the way to numerous, in fact, countless blessings.

One of my own blocks to receiving the Father's love was the unresolved pain from the verbally abusive relationship with my earthly father and the fact that I had never felt like I had received his blessing. Just before he died, when he was hospitalized, he had two dreams that he could not understand. He knew that I knew something about dreams. I had returned from a Spirit-filled mission trip to Southeast Asia and my dad had rallied and was now back at his home in rural Missouri. He sent word to me to come for a personal time just with him to talk about his haunting dreams.

The dreams themselves were rather detailed, but by the grace of God I understood their message and purpose. They showed some conditions that needed to be met before my dad could be released to go home to heaven and his concern for his family that would be left behind. Together alone, my dad let down his guard, which had never happened with me before. He told me stories of his growing up, of the abuse that he had suffered. I was shocked at his emotional transparency.

Then, with a tear coming down his cheek, he looked at me and said, "I've never understood you all your life." That took all of his courage to say. It was no news to me, because I had known that all along, but it was good for him to get it off his chest. And he asked me, "How did you get so close to God? Did you just press into Jesus, or what?"

In response, I told him a story. I said, "You know, I was told a story growing up that there was a woman who had a miscarriage and lost a little boy. She prayed and told God that if He would give her another son, she would dedicate him to His service. . . ."

Now there was a tear coming down my dad's other cheek. From his heart he said, "That story is true. That story is about you."

Then for the next five minutes, I experienced a kind of supernatural activity that I had never experienced before in my life. I felt a warmth, an absolute energy field, moving from his heart to mine. It was very tangible for five whole minutes. I actually felt fathered for the first time in my life. We joined hands. I prayed out loud. He did not pray out loud, but that was okay; he prayed for me silently. We blessed one another. That day he called me "Son" and I called him "Father." I have never been the same since then. That was the day I received my father's blessing and that was the day I began to become a father in the faith, which is so much more than being a minister of the faith or servant of the Lord.

Since then, I am able to bless people with a measure of that which God gave me. I can say to you through this printed page: "Your father understands you." Your Father in heaven understands your frame, your makeup, your weaknesses, your strengths, your idiosyncrasies, your failures, your limitations, your uncertainties and your insecurities. I can speak a father's blessing over you as you read these words (and remember, a blessing is always greater than the power of any dark curse).

May the invisible hand of God come upon you right now to heal your broken heart, to set you at liberty, to release you from every demonic stronghold. May the blood of Jesus cleanse you from all sin. May you know that you bring pleasure to His heart. In the name of the Father, the Son and the Holy Spirit, may blessings permeate the depths of your being. May you be at liberty to walk out of every darkness, now and in the future.

Firming Up Your Freedom

As you bask in the Father's presence, humble yourself and repent, confessing and disclosing and forsaking all past sins of commission and omission (see Proverbs 28:13; Mark 6:12–13; Acts 19:18). Forgive once again anybody who has harmed you (see Matthew 18:34–35). If necessary, resolve to make restitution and to seek reconciliation (see Luke 19:7–10; Matthew 5:23–25). Submit to God your Father as never before, making His Son, Jesus, the Lord of *all* (see Philippians 2:10–11). Destroy any object that would lure you away from Him (see Acts 19:19). Commit to walk in the light with fellow children of God, helping each other stay in the light (see John 3:19–21; Ephesians 5:8–14; 1 John 1:5–9).

Identify and Close Your Doors

As you secure your stance as the beloved of the Father, you can check yourself in another way that my friend Andy Reese calls the "four doors."[35] (This approach was developed during the revivals in Argentina and brought to the United States in various forms, where it has been modified further.)

As you would in your annual physical or a spring cleaning, you can look to make sure that these "doors" are closed before you assume that you are walking in the light. These doors are access points for darkness:

1. Sexual sin and soul ties
2. Anger and unforgiveness
3. Fear and control
4. Occult or false religion

As four key areas of sin, they must be closed (through repentance, forgiveness and the like) to shut out both demonic influences and the consequences of the sin in a person's life. Call on Jesus (see Joel 2:32) and you shall be delivered.

Weapons during Deliverance

Again as a review, do not forget to use your spiritual weaponry, which includes the following:

- The high praises of God (see Psalm 149:1, 5–9)
- The blood of Jesus (see Revelation 12:11)
- The name of Jesus (see Mark 16:17)
- Pronouncing forgiveness on behalf of others (see John 20:21–23)
- Resting in God (patience starves out the devil) (see Isaiah 26:3)

How to Keep Deliverance

As you walk in the light of the Father's love with other believers, keep "short accounts" with God and others, pray and fast regularly, read the Word of God, follow Jesus in everything you do and live by the power of His Holy Spirit. Then you will be walking in freedom. Your conversations will reflect the mentality of a conqueror—humble and confident at the same time, and able to bring God's help to others.

Having shifted from being a victim to being a victor, you will be able to speak life wherever you go. You will be able to achieve and maintain your freedom without incessant battles and misery. In fact, you will know when it is best to rest instead of engaging the enemy at all. You will discover that often the enemy will not bother you when you are resting in Jesus, gathering strength and enjoying the anointing oil of intimacy.

God's purpose in your struggles is never merely your survival, but rather your advancement. Your pain is a passageway to purity. Like a brightly colored butterfly, you are in metamorphosis—or maybe you have just emerged from your dark chrysalis! Yes, deliverance can be made easy when you bask in the reality of the Father's amazing love!

With the apostle Paul, allow me to bless you with a benediction that provides a highway leading out of darkness and into the brilliant heavenly light of the Father's throne:

194

Grace be to you and peace from God the Father, and from our Lord Jesus Christ, who gave himself for our sins, that he might deliver us from this present evil world, according to the will of God and our Father: to whom be glory for ever and ever. Amen.

Galatians 1:3–5, KJV

Receive now the free gift of the love of God through Christ Jesus the Lord. All things are possible—this is the place where light shines and darkness flees. You shall know the truth, and the truth shall set you free! May the truths contained in this book be used to help set the captives free. Always remember: whom the Son sets free, is free indeed!

Blessings to you,
James W. Goll

Appendix 1

A Brief History of Demonology in Quotes

The first Christians knew of the existence of dark spiritual beings at work behind the scenes under the rule of a high-ranking spiritual prince. The Son of God became man to destroy the demons (see 1 John 3:8), and by the authority of His Holy Spirit, the apostles and the early Church drove them out. Much more was and is at stake than the healing and betterment of individual people. The vital issue is the purification of the earth's whole atmosphere, the freeing of the entire social and political life, the total victory over our present world age, which is ruled by the princely power of the evil one.

In his book, *The Early Christians*, Eberhard Arnold wrote:

> The Christian alone has power over the raging enemy and its host,* because he reveals the supreme power of Christ, which the demonic powers have to acknowledge.** For every believing Christian is capable of unmasking demons and no demon can resist his command or persist in any lie. The demons must surrender to the servants of God because they fear Christ in God

197

and God in Christ. In fear, anger, and pain, they abandon their hold when the Crucified is proclaimed.***1

From the Early Church

Clement I of Rome, first century:

About A.D. 94–97, Clement I, bishop of Rome, wrote a letter to the church of Corinth, which had become severely factionalized. He expressed hope that the factions would be reconciled and seek forgiveness for the sins they had committed "through the promptings of the adversary." Here the Devil is perceived as a distinct personality urging the Christian community to sin and dissension.2

Ignatius of Antioch:

The letters of Saint Ignatius, bishop of Antioch, who was to be martyred in 107, indicate his . . . concern for order and unity in the Christian community. Influenced by Paul and showing similarities with the work of John, Ignatius saw the Devil as "ruler of this age". . . . Christ will introduce . . . a new age to be characterized by a radical transformation of the very nature of the world and its inhabitants. In this new kingdom, . . . evil will have no power. . . . Ignatius warned the Ephesians to evade the "stench" of the prince of this world, lest he divert them from the life that Christ wishes for them. The Devil's purpose is to thwart Christ's work of salvation by diverting the Christian people from their proper goal. Ignatius warned the Christians at Rome that the Devil pits himself against each person individually.3

Tertullian (c. A.D. 160–220):

According to Tertullian (*Apology* 46) Christian testimony is proved to be true by the following: first, the antiquity of the divine writings and the evidence of faith found in them; second,

·the acknowledgment of Christ by vanquished demonic powers. In other words, faith in the truth of the ancient Bible and
in Christ's power over demons had a crucial and convincing
significance for Tertullian.[4]

Justin Martyr (c. A.D. 100–165):

He has the power to drive away every importunate, evil angel and
to stop him from taking possession of our souls. . . . Therefore
God teaches us through his son to fight to the utmost for justice
and, when we come toward the close of life, to pray that our souls
may not fall into the hands of any of these evil powers.

Justin, *Dialogue with Trypho the Jew*, 105.3, 5; 106.1[5]

For every demon is exorcised, conquered, and subdued in the
very name of this Son of God, the firstborn of all creation, who
became man through a virgin, who suffered and was crucified
by your people under Pontius Pilate, who died and rose from
the dead and ascended into heaven.

Justin, *Dialogue with Trypho the Jew*, 85.1–2[6]

Around 150, St. Justin reveals that during their days of liturgical
preparation (preparation for baptism and entrance to community
life) catechumens (those learning Christ's way in preparation
for baptism) are taught "to pray and beseech God, in fasting, to
forgive all their past sins, while we pray and fast with them."

According to the testimony of Hippolytus and Tertullian, this
preparation seems to have lasted for one week, accompanied by
repeated exorcisms. These daily exorcisms took place during the
time of immediate preparation for baptism, which in the time
of Hippolytus lasted for one week.[7]

Hippolytus of Rome (c. A.D. 170–236):

The new ones to be accepted [catechumens who want to be
baptized] are questioned by the teachers about the reason for

their decision before they hear the Word. Those who bring them shall say whether they are ready for it and what their situation is. . . . Whoever has a demon needs purification before he takes part in the instruction. The professions and trades of those who are going to be accepted into the community must be examined. The nature and type of each must be established. . . . A magician shall not come up for examination either. An enchanter, an astrologer, a diviner, a soothsayer, a seducer of the people, one who practices magic with pieces of clothing, one who speaks in demonic riddles, one who makes amulets: all these shall desist or be rejected.

Hippolytus, Apostolic Tradition[8]

As another rite of exorcism we may include the anointing with oil . . . after the renunciation of Satan and just before the baptism. Hippolytus calls this "the oil of exorcism," and that the one administering it should say the words, "May every evil spirit depart from you."[9]

From the Desert Fathers (fourth and fifth centuries A.D.)

Antony the Great (A.D. 251–363):

[The devil] attempted to lead Antony away from the discipline, suggesting memories of his possessions, the guardianship of his sister, the bonds of kinship, love of money and of glory, the manifold pleasure of food, the relaxations of life, and finally, the rigor of virtue, and how great the labor is that earns it, suggesting also the bodily weakness and the length of time involved. So he raised in his mind a great dust cloud of considerations, since he wished to cordon him off from his righteous intention. But the enemy saw his own weakness in the face of Antony's resolve and saw that he instead was being thrown for a fall by the sturdiness of this contestant, and being overturned by his great faith and falling over Antony's constant prayers.[10]

This story continues on to show how evil thoughts and sensual temptations are overcome by prayer, faith, fasting and meditation on Christ. To banish thoughts of ease and love of pleasure, Antony meditated on the eternal judgment. The story also illustrates how demons take on shapes. A spirit of fornication took shape and began to accuse Antony, but Antony overcame him by the confession of the Word ("The Lord is my helper, and I shall look upon my enemies," from Psalm 118:7), which caused the enemy to flee.[11]

Isidore (c. A.D. 340):

["Abba" means "Father"] A brother asked Abba Isidore, "Why are the demons so frightened of you?" The old man said to him, "Because I have practiced asceticism since the day I became a monk, and not allowed anger to reach my lips."[12]

Evagrios the Solitary (c. A.D. 345–399):

A disciple of the Cappadocian Fathers, he was ordained reader by St. Basil the Great and deacon by St. Gregory the Theologian (Gregory of Nazianzos), and he accompanied the latter to the Council of Constantinople in 381. He went in 383 to Egypt where he spent the remaining sixteen years of his life. In Nitria, where he became a monk, he moved to the more remote desert of Kellia, dying there in 399. He knew both St. Makarios of Alexandria and St. Makarios the Egyptian and in them came into contact with the first generation of the Desert Fathers and with their spirituality in its purest form.[13]

Evagrios noted that weapons against lust were fasting and vigils, and against anger were long-suffering, forbearance, forgiveness and compassionate acts. He said that prayer would purify the intellect. Other demons he noted included rancor, self-esteem (which is overcome by intense prayer and by not doing or saying anything that contributes to the sense of your own importance) and the deluder (which gets us overbusy so as not to have strength to resist other demons like unchastity, anger, or dejection). "There is scarcely any other virtue which the demons fear as much as gentleness (meekness)."[14]

Evagrios gave several classifications of demons. He identified the front-line demons as those being opposed to spiritual growth. He enumerated three types: those responsible for gluttony and sensuality, those responsible for avaricious thought, and those which led one to seek the esteem of men. He derived these classifications from the temptations which Jesus overcame in Matthew 4:1–10. Evagrios believed that other demons then followed after these had their success.[15]

Arsenius (c. A.D. 360–449):

It happened that when Abba Arsenius was sitting in his cell that he was harassed by demons. His servants, on their return, stood outside his cell and heard him praying to God in these words, "O God, do not leave me. I have done nothing good in your sight, but according to your goodness, let me now make a beginning of good."[16]

Moses (c. A.D. 350):

It happened that Abba Moses was struggling with the temptation of fornication. Unable to stay any longer in the cell, he went and told Abba Isidore. The old man exhorted him to return to his cell. But he refused, saying, "Abba, I cannot." Then Abba Isidore took Moses out onto the terrace and said to him, "Look towards the west." He looked and saw hordes of demons flying about and making a noise before launching an attack. Then Abba Isidore said to him, "Look towards the east." He turned and saw an innumerable multitude of holy angels shining with glory. Abba Isidore said, "See, these are sent by the Lord to the saints to bring them help, while those in the west fight against them. Those who are with us are more in number than they are." Then Abba Moses gave thanks to God, plucked up courage and returned to his cell.[17]

John Cassian (c. A.D. 360–435):

As a young man, John Cassian joined a monastery in Bethlehem, but around 385–386, he traveled with a friend to Egypt, where he remained until 399, becoming a disciple of Evagrios. During 401–405 he was at Constantinople, where he was ordained deacon and became a disciple of John Chrysostom. In 405, he traveled to the west, spending a number of years in Rome, then moving to Gaul, at some point being ordained priest. Around 415, he founded two monasteries near Marseilles, one for men and one for women.

In his essay, "On the Eight Vices," Cassian enumerates eight demons connected with eight vices. These are: gluttony, unchastity (the desire of the flesh), avarice (greed), anger, dejection, listlessness (laziness, distraction), self-esteem (self-centeredness), and pride. "The fathers also say that as a rule someone who works is attacked and afflicted but by a single demon, while someone who does not work is taken prisoner by a thousand evil spirits."[18]

As a safeguard against pride, Cassian recommends: "When we have attained some degree of holiness, we should always repeat to ourselves the words of the Apostle, 'Yet not I, but the grace of God which was in me' (1 Cor. 15:10), as well as what was said by the Lord: 'Without me you can do nothing' (John 15:5). . . . and finally: 'It does not depend on man's will or effort, but on God's mercy' (Rom. 9:16)."[19]

Agathon (c. A.D. 370):

The brethren also asked him, "Amongst all good works, which is the virtue which requires the greatest effort?" He answered, "Forgive me, but I think there is no labor greater than that of prayer to God. For every time a man wants to pray, his enemies,

203

the demons, want to prevent him, for they know that it is only by turning him from prayer that they can hinder his journey. Whatever good work a man undertakes, if he perseveres in it, he will attain rest. But prayer is warfare to the last breath."[20]

Theodore of Pherme (c. A.D. 370):

It was said of Abba Theodore that when he settled down at Scetis, a demon came to him wanting to enter his cell, but he bound him to the outside of his cell. Once more another demon tried to enter, and he bound him too. A third demon came as well, and finding the other two bound, said to them, "Why are you standing outside like this?" They said to him, "He is sitting inside and will not let us enter." So the demon tried to enter by force. The old man bound him too. Fearing the prayers of the old man, they begged him, saying, "Let us go," and the old man said to them, "Go away." Then they went off covered with confusion.[21]

Elias (c. A.D. 400):

Abba Elias said, "I saw someone who was carrying a skin of wine on his arm, and in order to make the demons blush, for it was a fantasy, I said to the brother, 'Of your charity, take off your cloak.' He took off his cloak and was not found to be carrying anything. I say that so that you may not believe even what you see or hear. Even more, observe your thoughts and beware of what you have in your heart and your spirit, knowing that the demons put ideas into you so as to corrupt your soul by making it think that which is not right, in order to turn your spirit from the consideration of your sins and of God."[22]

Longinus (c. A.D. 407):

Another time, they brought him one possessed by a demon. He said to those who were escorting him: "I can do nothing for you; but go instead to Abba Zeno." So Abba Zeno began to put pressure onto the demon to cast it out. The demon began to cry out: "Perhaps, Abba Zeno, you think I am going away because of you; look, down there Abba Longinus is praying, and challenging me and it is for fear of his prayers that I go away, for to you I would not even have given an answer."[23]

Poemen (c. A.D. 407):

Abba Joseph put the same question [on the subject of impure thoughts] and Abba Poemen said to him, "If someone shuts a snake and a scorpion up in a bottle, in time they will be completely destroyed. So it is with evil thoughts: they are suggested by the demons; they disappear through patience."[24]

Francis of Assisi (1181 or 1182–1226):

Once, at the Place of Portiuncula, when St. Francis was praying devoutly, by divine revelation he saw the whole place surrounded and besieged by devils, as by a great army. But not one of them was able to enter into the place because the friars were so holy that the devils could find no one to whom they could gain admittance. . . .

And so [Francis] went forth through divers regions, boldly preaching the Gospel, the Lord working with him and confirming his word by signs following. And in the power of his Name, Francis, the herald of the truth, cast forth devils, healed the sick, and, what is more, by the efficacy of his word softened the most hardened hearts and brought them to penance, restoring at the same time the health of the body and the soul.[25]

The Reformers

Martin Luther (1483–1546):

Martin Luther devoted more theological and personal concern to the Devil than anyone else since the desert fathers. For Luther any valid view must rest upon the Bible read in the light of faith.[26]

205

Luther felt this struggle intensely within his own soul. His diabology [study of the devil] was based on personal experience as well as on Scripture and tradition. . . . Like the desert fathers and the medieval contemplatives, Luther felt that the Devil attacks more intensely as one advances in faith. Satan attempted to deter him from God's work through temptations, distractions, and even physical manifestations. . . .

Yet Satan's power over us is shattered by the Incarnation of Jesus Christ. . . . The world, the flesh, and the Devil still tempt us, but one little word—the name of the Savior—can crush them. . . .

The Devil's power remains "as big as the world, as wide as the world, and he extends from heaven down into hell," yet "the evil spirit has not a hairbreadth more power over us than God's goodness permits." Against the Devil, Christ puts a great arsenal at the disposal of Christians, including baptism, the Bible, preaching, the sacraments, and song. Luther's best known contribution to popular diabology is his famous hymn; "A Mighty Fortress is Our God."[27]

John Calvin (1509–1564):

John Calvin, another great Protestant reformer, offered a precise, rational statement of his views in *The Institutes of Christian Religion.* . . . Calvin shared Luther's view of God's total omnipotence. No fate, fortune, chance, or freedom limits this complete sovereignty. Why God ordains evil is a mystery that we are not permitted to unravel. Yet, Calvin insisted, God has only one united will; although he seems to our limited intelligence to do both good and evil, he always works for the ultimate good. God not only permits evil; he actively wills it, as when he turned Pharaoh over to the Evil One to be confirmed in his obstinacy. In every evil human act, three forces are working together: the human will to sin, the Devil's will to evil, and God's will to the ultimate good. In every evil person, Satan and the Lord are both at work for their own purpose.

206

The Devil's role in such a theology was similar to that in Luther's. Calvin firmly rejected the skeptical view that angels and demons are only human ideas. Still, he did not pay nearly as much attention to the Evil One as his German colleague did. Recognizing that the Bible offers few particulars on the Devil, Calvin insisted that a detailed diabology [study of the devil] was inappropriate. Since he experienced the Devil's assaults less personally than Luther, Calvin assigned him a narrower place in the world. Satan is completely under God's command and cannot do any evil that God does not expressly assign him. "To carry out his judgment through Satan as the minister of his wrath, God destines men's purposes as he pleases, arouses their wills, and strengthens their endeavors."[28]

The Quakers and George Fox (1624–1691):

George Fox began the Society of Friends, later known as the Quakers, in about 1647. The early Friends were known for healing and deliverance. George Fox kept a "Book of Miracles" to record such events.

"When I was a prisoner in the same place there came a woman to me to the prison and two with her and said that she had been possessed two and thirty years. And the priests had kept her and had kept fasting days about her and could not do her any good. And she said the Lord said unto her, 'Arise for I have a sanctified people. Haste, and go to them, for thy redemption draweth nigh.' [So when Fox was released from prison, he had her come to meetings.] . . . And the poor woman would make such a noise in roaring and sometimes lying along upon her belly upon the ground and with her spirit and roaring and voice, and would set all Friends in a heat and sweat.

"And I said, 'All Friends keep to your own, lest that which is in her get into you.' And so she affrighted the world from our meetings. And then they said if that were cast out of her while she was with us, and were made well, then they would say that we were of God. This said the world, and I had said before that she should be set free.

"And then it was upon me that we should have a meeting at Skegby at Elizabeth Hooton's house, when we had her there. And there were many Friends almost overcome by her with the stink that came out of her, roaring and tumbling on the ground. And the same day she was worse than ever she was, and then another day we met about her, and about the first hour the life rose in Friends, and said it was done and she rose up and her countenance changed and became white and before it was wan and earthly. And she sat down at my thigh as I was sitting and lift up her hands and said, 'Ten thousand praise the Lord,' and did not know where she was, and so she was well."[29]

Appendix 2

Common Demonic Groupings

Note that these categories and names should not be considered restrictive; they are meant to provide a general idea of how groups of demons function together, often under a "strongman."

Accusation
Judging
Criticism
Faultfinding
Perfectionism
Religion

Addictions and Compulsions
Nicotine
Alcohol
Drugs
Caffeine
Gluttony
Pornography

Affectation
Theatrics
Playacting
Sophistication
Pretension
Performance

Bitterness
Resentment
Hatred
Unforgiveness
Violence
Temper
Anger
Retaliation

Revenge
Murder

Competition
Drivenness
Argument
Pride
Jealousy
Ego

Confusion
Forgetfulness
Frustration
Incoherence
Deaf and dumb spirits
Double-mindedness

209

Control
Possessiveness
Dominance
Witchcraft
Jezebel

Covetousness
Stealing
Kleptomania
Material lust
Greed
Discontent

Cults
Jehovah's Witnesses
Christian Science
Rosicrucianism
Theosophy
Urantia
Subud, Latihan
Unity
Mormonism
Bahaism
Unitarianism
Also lodges, societies,
social agencies that use
the Bible and God as a
basis but omit the blood
atonement of Jesus
Christ

Cursing
Blasphemy
Coarse jesting
Gossip
Railing
Criticism
Sarcasm
Backbiting
Mockery
Belittling

Death
Suicide
Death wish

Fear of death
Murder
Abortion

Depression
Despair
Despondency
Discouragement
Defeatism
Dejection
Hopelessness
Suicide
Death
Insomnia
Morbidity

Doubt
Unbelief
Skepticism
Self-doubt

Escape
Indifference
Stoicism
Passivity
Sleepiness
Alcohol
Drugs
Addiction

False Burden
False responsibility
False compassion
Codependency
Messiah complex

False Religions
Buddhism
Taoism
Hinduism
Islam
Shintoism
Confucianism
(many others)

Fatigue
Tiredness
Weariness
Laziness

Fear of Authority
Lying
Deceit
Rebellion
Fear of rejection
Ahab

Fears (All Kinds)
Phobias (all kinds)
Hysteria

Gluttony
Idleness
Nervousness
Compulsive eating
Resentment
Frustration
Self-pity
Self reward

Grief
Sorrow
Heartache
Heartbreak
Sadness
Cruelty

Guilt
Condemnation
Shame
Unworthiness
Embarrassment

Impatience
Agitation
Frustration
Intolerance
Resentment
Criticism

Indecision
Compromise
Procrastination
Confusion
Forgetfulness
Indifference
Passivity

Infirmity
Weakness
(any disease or sickness)

Inheritance
*Evil spirits passed
down from parents to
children:*
(physical)
(emotional)
(mental)
(curses)

Insecurity
Rejection
Orphan spirits
Inferiority
Self-pity
Loneliness
Timidity
Shyness
Inadequacy
Ineptness

Heaviness
False burden
Disgust
Gloom
Despair
Depression

Hyperactivity
Restlessness
Drivenness
Pressure

Jealousy
Selfishness
Envy
Suspicion
Distrust

Mental Illness
Insanity
Madness
Mania
Retardation
Senility
Schizophrenia
Paranoia
Hallucinations
Alzheimer's disease

Mind-Binding
Confusion
Fear of man
Fear of failure
Occult spirits
Spiritism spirits

Mind Idolatry
Analytical skepticism
Intellectualism
Rationalization
Pride
Ego
Deaf and dumb spirits

Nervousness
Tension
Headache
Nervous habits
Restlessness
Excitement
Insomnia
Roving spirits

Occult
Witchcraft
Conjuration

Charms
Fetishes
Ouija board
Palmistry
Handwriting analysis
Automatic handwriting
ESP
Hypnotism
Horoscope
White/black magic
Astrology
Levitation
Fortune-telling
Water-witching
Séance
Tarot cards
Pendulum
Incantation
(others)

Paranoia
Jealousy
Envy
Suspicion
Distrust
Persecution
Fears
Confrontation

Passivity
Indifference
Listlessness
Lethargy
Religion

Perfection
Anger
Pride
Vanity
Ego
Frustration
Criticism
Irritability
Intolerance

Persecution

Unfairness
Fear of judgment
Fear of reproof
Fear of accusation
Sensitiveness

Pride

Self-righteousness
Ego
Vanity
Haughtiness
Fear of condemnation
Arrogance
Greed

Rebellion

Self-will
Stubbornness
Disobedience
Independence
Anti-submissiveness
Witchcraft

Religion

Ritualism
Formalism
Legalism
Doctrinal obsession
Seduction
Doctrinal error
Terror
Passivity
Fear of lost salvation
Religiosity
Poverty
(others)

Rejection

Self-rejection
Fear of rejection

Abuse
Self-hatred
Retaliation
Abandonment
Orphan spirits

Retaliation

Destruction
Spite
Hatred
Cruelty
Sadism
Hurt
Murder

Self-Accusation

Self-hatred
Self-condemnation
Self-rejection
Orphan
Cutting

Self-Deception

Self-delusion
Self-seduction
Pride

Sensitiveness

Self-awareness
Fear of man
Fear of disapproval
Fear of rejection
Paranoia

Sexual Impurity

Lust
Fantasy lust
Compulsive
Masturbation
Homosexuality

Lesbianism
Adultery
Fornication
Immorality
Incest
Harlotry
Rape
Frigidity
Pornography

Spiritism

Séance
Spirit guide
Necromancy
Familiar spirits
Deception
(others)

Strife

Contention
Bickering
Argument
Quarreling
Fighting
Greed

Withdrawal

Pouting
Daydreaming
Fantasy
Pretension
Unreality

Worry

Anxiety
Fear
Dread
Apprehension
Poverty

212

Notes

Chapter 1: Jesus, Overcoming Demons

1. The picture of Jesus, first at His baptism in the Jordan and immediately afterward in the trackless wasteland that was home to evil spirits, is portrayed in Matthew 3:13–4:11; Mark 1:9–13; Luke 3:21–22 and 4:1–15.

2. Just as there are angels who are in authority over other angels (the "arch" in archangel means "ruler"), so there are evil principalities who rule over lesser ones. The Pharisees and some Jewish exorcists believed that if you knew the demon's name you had authority over it. This is not always true, but it is reflected in this story. The real source of authority is in the name of Jesus.

3. The apostle Paul wrote: "And since we have the same spirit of faith, according to what is written [in Psalm 116:10], 'I believed and therefore I spoke,' we also believe and therefore speak" (2 Corinthians 4:13).

4. "I will return to my house from which I came" (Matthew 12:44, NASB). "For you have said in your heart: 'I will ascend into heaven, I will exalt my throne above the stars of God. . . . I will be like the Most High'" (Isaiah 14:13–14).

5. "You believe that God is one; you do well. So do the demons believe and shudder [in terror and horror such as make a man's hair stand on end and contract the surface of his skin]!" (James 2:19, AMP).

Chapter 2: Overcoming Demons in the Early Church

1. "The evil spirit answered and said, 'Jesus I know, and Paul I know; but who are you?'" (Acts 19:15).

2. Why then did the apostles sometimes disobey civil authorities? When they did so, it was with a submissive spirit. Peter and John were brought before the Sanhedrin and forbidden to preach the Gospel (see Acts 5:29–42). They rightly said, "We must obey God rather than men." But they received submissively the punishment assigned to them for making that decision.

3. Because our "kingdom is not of this world" (John 18:36), we are to be submissive to earthly rulers while resisting their counterparts in heavenly places. This

illustrates the importance of recognizing the earthly counterparts of the satanic, princely realm. Behind the human prince of Tyre in Ezekiel 28:2 was the fallen angel king of Tyre in verse 12. Elsewhere in Scripture, the phrase "principalities and powers" can refer either to earthly rulers (see Titus 3:1; Romans 13:1) or their satanic counterparts (see Ephesians 6:12; 1 Corinthians 2:6–8).

4. John the Baptist, Stephen and all the apostles are referred to as witnesses or martyrs in Mark 6:14–29; Acts 7:54–60; John 21:18–19 and 2 Timothy 4:6–8.

Chapter 3: Scriptural Characteristics of Demons

1. In most English versions of the Bible, the term "unclean spirit(s)" is used twenty-two times.

2. (To *have* a demon) see Matthew 11:18; Mark 7:25; 9:17; Luke 4:33; 8:27; 13:11; John 7:20; 8:49, 52; 10:20–21.

3. (To be *in*, or *under the influence of* a demon) see Mark 1:23; 5:2.

4. (To be *demonized*) see Matthew 4:24; 8:16, 28, 33; 9:32; 12:22; 15:22; Mark 1:32; 5:15–16, 18; Luke 8:36.

Chapter 4: Truths and Tactics of Temptation

1. Sam Storms, "Tactics of Temptation," posted on the Enjoying God Ministries website (November 8, 2006), http://www.enjoyinggodministries.com/article/tactics-of-temptation/ (accessed April 14, 2009). Dr. Sam Storms collaborated with me in developing the early material for this chapter.

2. William Gurnall, *The Christian in Complete Armour*, Moody Press edition (Lindale, Tex.: World Challenge, Inc., 1986), 39.

3. Neil T. Anderson, *The Bondage Breaker* (Eugene, Ore.: Harvest House, 1993), 126–128.

Chapter 5: Battle Plans for Overcomers

1. Starting out as earthbound caterpillars, it is as if we are now in a dark chrysalis, dying to our old, carnal selves so that we can emerge into the light of a new day as completely new creatures. There are several states in metamorphosis; one of them is actually called liquification. Before the butterfly can emerge, all of the traces of the old creature need to be melted down and recombined. This is a drastic exchange, and it mirrors the transformation that occurs when we submit to the Lordship of Jesus Christ.

Chapter 7: Realms of Kingdom Authority

1. Eberhard Arnold, *The Early Christians* (Farmington, Penn.: Plough Publishing House, 2007), 27–28 (Also available online at: http://www.plough.com/ebooks/pdfs/EarlyChristians.pdf.).

2. See, for example, Heidi and Rolland Baker's book, *Expecting Miracles: True Stories of God's Supernatural Power and How You Can Experience It* (Grand Rapids: Chosen, 2007), 101–2. Also see Heidi Baker and Shara Pradhan, *Compelled*

by Love: How to Change the World through the Simple Power of Love in Action (Lake Mary, Fla.: Charisma House, 2008), 115–116.

Chapter 8: Preparations for Deliverance

1. Frank and Ida Mae Hammond, *Pigs in the Parlor: A Practical Guide to Deliverance* (Kirkwood, Mo.: Impact Christian Books, Inc., 1973, 2008), 77–78.

Chapter 9: Effective Procedures for Deliverance

1. John Loren Sandford and Mark Sandford, *Deliverance and Inner Healing* (Grand Rapids: Chosen Books, 1992, 2008), 175–176.

2. See chapter 4 in *Biblical Healing and Deliverance: A Guide to Experiencing Freedom from Sins of the Past, Destructive Beliefs, Emotional and Spiritual Pain, Curses and Oppression* by Chester and Betsy Kylstra (Grand Rapids: Chosen Books, 2005). Another great resource on this topic from Chester and Betsy Kylstra is chapter 8 in *Restoring the Foundations: An Integrated Approach to Healing Ministry*, 2nd ed. (Pomona, N.J.: Proclaiming His Word, 2001).

Chapter 10: Curses: Causes and Cures

1. For examples of the types of repercussions that can result from involvement with Freemasonry, see Ron G. Campbell, *Free from Freemasonry: Understanding "the Craft" and How It Affects Those You Love* (Ventura, Calif.: Gospel Light Publications, 1999), 168ff.

2. See Galatians 3:13–14; Ephesians 1:7; Colossians 1:13–14, 1 John 3:8; Luke 10:19.

3. See Hebrews 3:1; Romans 10:10.

4. "Has the Lord as much delight in burnt offerings and sacrifices as in obeying the voice of the Lord? Behold, to obey is better than sacrifice, and to heed than the fat of rams" (1 Samuel 15:22, NASB).

5. "He who covers his sins will not prosper, but whoever confesses and forsakes them will have mercy" (Proverbs 28:13).

6. See Mark 11:25; Matthew 6:12–13.

7. See Leviticus 19:26; Deuteronomy 7:25–26; 18:10–11; Acts 19:18–20.

8. "So be subject to God. Resist the devil [stand firm against him], and he will flee from you" (James 4:7, AMP).

Chapter 11: Generational Blessings

1. Gary Smalley and John Trent, *The Blessing* (Nashville: Thomas Nelson, 2004).

Chapter 12: Deliverance Made Easy

1. I am indebted to my friend Andy Reese for his portrayal of the Father's love in his Scripture-based "letter" from God the Father entitled "My Child . . ." You

can find it in his book, *Freedom Tools for Overcoming Life's Tough Problems* (Grand Rapids: Chosen Books, 2008), 43–46.

2. See Ephesians 1:3–12.

3. See Psalm 139:15–16.

4. See Psalm 139:1.

5. See Psalm 139:2–3.

6. See Matthew 10:29–31.

7. See Jeremiah 1:4–5.

8. See Psalm 139:13–14.

9. See Psalm 71:6; Acts 17:26.

10. See Acts 17:28.

11. See Genesis 1:27.

12. See 1 John 3:1.

13. See Matthew 5:48.

14. See 1 John 4:16; John 8:41–44.

15. See Matthew 6:31–33; 7:11; James 1:17.

16. See Jeremiah 32:41.

17. See 1 John 13:1.

18. See Jeremiah 31:3; 32:40; John 17:26.

19. See Exodus 19:5; Jeremiah 29:11.

20. See Jeremiah 33:3.

21. See Philippians 2:13.

22. See Deuteronomy 4:29; Psalm 37:4.

23. See Ephesians 3:20.

24. See Psalm 139:17–18.

25. See Zephaniah 3:17.

26. See 2 Thessalonians 2:16–17.

27. See Hebrews 1:3; Romans 8:31.

28. See 1 John 4:10; 2 Corinthians 5:18–19.

29. 2 Corinthians 1:3–4; Revelation 21:3–4.

30. See Psalm 34:18; Isaiah 40:11.

31. See Romans 8:38–39.

32. See Psalm 103:17.

33. See Luke 15:22–32.

34. For more on the subject of soul ties, refer to the lesson titled, "Breaking Emotional Bondages" in my study guide, *The Healing Anointing*, one of the resources available on my Encounters Network website: http://www.encounter snetwork.com.

35. See Reese, *Freedom Tools*, 178.

Appendix 1: A Brief History of Demonology in Quotes

1. Eberhard Arnold, *The Early Christians* (Farmington, Penn.: Plough Publishing House, 2007), 37 [e-book: http://www.plough.com/ebooks/pdfs/Early Christians.pdf]. Quoting from * Cyprian, "To Donatus" 5. [*Epistles of Cyprian of Carthage*, "To Donatus," Letter 5]; ** Tertullian, *Apology* 46. [R. T. Glover, trans., *Tertullian: Apology* (Cambridge, Mass.: Harvard University Press, 1960)];***

Tertullian, *Apology* 27; Tatian, *Address to the Greeks*, 16 [Hinrichs, 1923, 1924, *Tatians Rede an die Griechen*, translated into German, Gessen, 1884].

2. Jeffery Burton Russell, *Satan: The Early Christian Tradition* (Ithaca, N.Y.: Cornell University Press, 1987), 33–34, quoting from Clement 51:1.

3. Ibid., 34–35.

4. Arnold, 53.

5. Ibid., 247.

6. Ibid., 88.

7. Michael Dujarier and Kevin Hart, trans., *The Rites of Christian Initiation* (New York: Sadlier, 1979), 94.

8. Arnold, 99.

9. Dujarier, 118.

10. Robert Gregg, trans., *Athanasius: The Life of Antony and the Letter to Marcellinus* (New York: Paulist Press, 1980), 33–34.

11. Ibid., 35.

12. Benedicta Ward, trans., *The Sayings of the Desert Fathers* (Kalamazoo, Mich.: Cistercian Publications, 1975), 99–97.

13. G. E. H. Palmer, et al., trans., *The Philokalia: The Complete Text (Vol. 1)* (London: Faber and Faber, 1979), 29.

14. *Philokalia*, 46.

15. Ibid., 52.

16. *Sayings*, 5.

17. Ibid., 138.

18. *Philokalia*, 90.

19. Ibid., 93.

20. *Sayings*, 21–22.

21. Ibid., 78.

22. Ibid., 71.

23. Ibid., 123.

24. Ibid., 170.

25. St. Bonaventure, *The Life of St. Francis of Assisi* (Rockford, Ill.: Tan Books, 1988), 117.

26. Jeffery Burton Russell, *The Prince of Darkness* (Ithaca, N.Y.: Cornell University Press, 1992), 170.

27. Ibid., 172.

28. Ibid., 173–74.

29. Henry J. Cadbury, ed., *George Fox's Book of Miracles* (Philadelphia: Quakers Uniting in Publications, 2000), 107.

Index

over sickness and death,
101–2
over temptations,
100–101
Kingdom of God, 14,
16, 17, 19, 38, 51, 69,
84, 85, 98, 102, 172,
178, 180

Laban, 171
license and licentious-
ness, 65–67
life, love of, 44–45
Longinus, 205
Luther, Martin, 206
Lydia, 32–34

martyrs, 44, 45
martus (martyr, witness),
44, 45, 214n4(ch. 2)
Michel, 162
Moses (c. A.D. 350), 202–3
Moses (Old Testament),
153–54, 159

Noah, 86
never quitting, 107–9,
109–12

Paul, 32–33, 34, 36, 39,
45, 158, 162–63,
213n3(ch. 1)
in Ephesus, 34
imprisonment of, 33–34
warnings of against re-
ligious spirits, 41
warnings of against se-
ducing spirits, 42
Peter, 31, 34, 158,
213n2(ch. 2)
on suffering, 37–38
Philip, 31–32, 34
Philippi, 32, 34
Pontius Pilate, 158
praising God, 81
prayers, of release and
thanksgiving, 165–66

Prince, Derek, 44, 118
principalities, 36
and early powers,
213–14n3

Quakers, 207–8

Rachel, 157
rebellion, 29, 37, 38, 54,
84, 116, 124–25
Reese, Andy, 193,
215n1(ch. 12)
repentance, 65, 113–15,
119, 120, 123, 141,
142, 193
Revelation, book of,
42–43
righteousness, 40, 41, 50,
55, 63, 69, 79, 110,
111, 114, 119
rights, legal and experi-
ential, 162–64
rulers of darkness, 36–37

Samaria, 31
Sandford, John Loren,
136
Sandford, Mark, 136
Satan, 30, 37, 45, 62,
64–65, 72, 93, 158
as fallen, 87–89
favorite tactics of,
75–76
goal of, 67
plan of overruled by
God, 83–85
staying free of his
snares, 40–41
when he tempts us,
77–79
why he tempts us, 75
Saul, king of Israel, 81
sexual immorality, 18, 40,
116, 117, 120–21, 134,
142, 154, 160
Silas, imprisonment of,
33–34

sin
the "four doors" of, 193
unconfessed, 190
See also sexual
immorality
Smalley, Gary, 173
sorcery, 118, 119
spiritual armor and
weapons, 39–40,
79–81
godly character, 40
prayer, 41
the Word of God, 41
See also righteousness
spiritual warfare in the
epistles, 36–38
spiritual wickedness, 37
Stephen, 31–32
Storms, Sam, 214n1(ch.
4)
suffering, 37–38

temptation, 62–63
tactics of, 64–65
tactics for resisting,
67–70
Tertullian, 198–99
Theodore of Pherme, 204
Transfiguration, the, 19
Trent, John, 173

"walled city" principle,
54–55
war
Book of the Wars of
the Lord, the, 72–73
Scriptures of, 73–75
watchfulness, 39–40,
41–42
Wesley, John, 41
witchcraft, 117, 118
witnessing, 44
Word of God, the, 79–81
"world system," 93

About the Author

J ames W. Goll is the cofounder of Encounters Network. James also acts as the director of Prayer Storm, an internet based virtual house of prayer. James is a member of the Harvest International Ministries Apostolic Team and is a contributing writer for *Kairos* magazine and other periodicals. James and Michal Ann were married for 32 years before her graduation into heaven in the fall of 2008, and together they had four wonderful children. James continues to live in the beautiful rolling hills of Franklin, Tennessee.

James has produced several study guides on subjects such as equipping in the prophetic, blueprints for prayer, and empowerment for ministry, all of which are available through the Encounters Resource Center.

Other books by James W. and Michal Ann Goll

365 Devotional Prayer Journal
Adventures in the Prophetic
Angelic Encounters
The Beginner's Guide to Hearing God
The Beginner's Guide to Signs, Wonders and the Supernatural Life
A Call to Courage
The Call to the Elijah Revolution
A Call to the Secret Place

The Coming Israel Awakening
The Coming Prophetic Revolution
Compassion: A Call to Take Action
Deliverance from Darkness
Deliverance from Darkness Study Guide
Discovering the Seer in You
Dream Language
Empowered Prayer
Empowered Women
Exploring the Gift and Nature of Dreams
God Encounters
Intercession: The Power and the Passion to Shape History
The Lost Art of Intercession
The Lost Art of Practicing His Presence
Prayer Storm
Prayer Storm Study Guide
Praying for Israel's Destiny
The Prophetic Intercessor
The Seer
The Seer Devotional Journal

For more information, contact:
Encounters Network
P.O. Box 1653
Franklin, TN 37057
Office phone: (615) 599-5552
Office fax: (615) 599-5554
For orders call: 1-877-200-1604

For more information or to sign up for monthly email communiqués, please visit www.encountersnetwork.com or send an email request to info@encountersnetwork.com.

For more information on Prayer Storm, visit www.prayer storm.com. You may sign up for an hour of prayer or view the weekly web broadcast by visiting this website.

Made in the USA
Coppell, TX
04 January 2022

70852975R00132